Inspiring Connection

Small Groups where Everyone Matters

Eddie Oliver

Life-Giving Conversations Press
Virginia Beach, Virginia
www.LifeGivingConversations.com

INSPIRING CONNECTION

Small Groups where Everyone Matters

The poem "Loaves and Fishes" by David Whyte on page 6 is reprinted with permission from Many Rivers Press.

"On Listening" by Ralph Roughton on page 68 is reprinted with permission from Friends Publishing Corporation.

The "loaves and fishes" logo appearing on pages 68, 74, 75 and 77 in the Appendix is used with the permission of a private charity in California: Sacramento Loaves & Fishes, Sister Libby Fernandez, Executive Director.

About the cover: The word cloud graphic is a relational summary of distinct themes and concepts in this book. Each theme has its own color. Words of the same color represent a rough grouping of concepts within that theme; the prominence of a concept is related to the size of the font. The word cloud was generated at www.textisbeautiful.net.

ISBN: 978-0692434345

Printed in the United States of America

Life-Giving Conversations Press

This book is dedicated to you and your small group.
May every group member experience the relief of meaningful connection
and the life-giving satisfaction of authentic community.

CONTENTS

(Continued on next page...)

FOREWORD

Churches in America are at a critical crossroads. Faced with aging and ever-smaller congregations, younger generations increasingly "spiritual but not religious," and traditional theology under siege, one thing is clear: Churches must change.

Though the classic Sunday service in which a pastor or minister delivers a sermon continues to be the centerpiece of church, alternatives and additions are being tested and tried. People today don't want to just sit and listen; they want to explore, engage, experience, and express. They want to dive deep into spiritual concepts and discover the Truth for themselves. They want to connect with others and learn from their wisdom. Though receptive to sermons, lessons and lectures, they also want to question, discuss, and reflect on their own.

How can churches meet these needs for their congregants? One of those most promising ways is small group ministry. Through this approach, small group members come together to discuss spiritual topics through the lens of their own personal ideas, experiences and questions. They forge meaningful bonds, grow individually and collectively, and together shape new insights. In this new role, the church is not responsible for providing answers, but for offering a structure through which individuals can discover their answers for themselves.

But where to begin? And how?

Fortunately, Eddie Oliver has "been there, done that" and, through this wonderful book, he makes it easy for the rest of us. His analysis is thorough, his detail, meticulous. There is no guess-work here: Eddie knows what works, and now, through his book, so do we.

You'll find in here not only the secrets to success for small groups, how to form and launch them, and how to enroll and train facilitators, but also a step-by-step guide for making sure each meeting goes smoothly and meets the needs of its participants. Wondering how to keep some people from monopolizing the conversation? The answers are here. How to graciously assure that the meeting starts and ends on time? See inside.

But wait! There's more: A whole Appendix full of forms, sample promotional materials, answers to frequently asked questions, and meeting templates as well as a section of useful hand-outs that you can use in your own small groups.

What a find!

Permeating all of it is Eddie's passion for small group ministry. Building on the idea of "breaking bread and serving one another," he offers us a clear path for building "authentic community and connection." It is a connection, he notes, for which we all hunger. Moreover, it is the underpinning of our spiritual journey: How we learn to let our own Divine light shine while appreciating that light in others.

Enjoy this book but more than anything: Put it to use. It will enhance the way you think of ministry, create new ways to re-engage the non-religious, and very possibly, change the course of your spiritual life.

Reverend Paula Mekdeci
Chesapeake, Virginia

Author's Note

In his book *The Different Drum,* psychiatrist M. Scott Peck made a compelling distinction between social association and authentic community:

> *We human beings have often been referred to as social animals. But we are not yet community creatures. We are impelled to relate with each other for our survival. But we do not yet relate with the inclusivity, realism, self-awareness, vulnerability, commitment, openness, freedom, equality, and love of genuine community. It is clearly no longer enough to be simply social animals, babbling together at cocktail parties and brawling with each other in business and over boundaries. It is our task—our essential, central, crucial task—to transform ourselves from mere social creatures into community creatures. It is the only way that human evolution will be able to proceed.*

Authentic community springs from one central, life-giving organizing principle: *Everyone belongs, everyone matters, everyone is a contribution.* This organizing principle is the soul of small group ministry that inspires connection.

The small group process you will read about in this book is the product of trial and error, collaboration, and co-creation with people in my own spiritual community who shared my heart's desire:

> *Our Vision: Everyone is connected.*
> *Our Mission: To enrich life, one small group at a time.*

I hope that you will benefit from the story of our pilgrimage from mere social fellowship to the sacredness of authentic community.

Eddie Oliver
Virginia Beach, Virginia
May 2015

How to Use this Book

Regardless of what type of small group you want to start or what small group program you want to enhance, begin with Part One of this book. The first thing you may notice about the group documented in Part One is that there is no curriculum, no video, no book, and no study guide. The focus is on one thing: creating authentic community. This is no ordinary social group. It is a small group with the shared intention of prioritizing meaningful connection among its participants. Gain an understanding of what works to cultivate authentic community—and what doesn't. Walk through the steps of organizing this small group program. Learn the all-inclusive details involved in training facilitators as well as the subtle nuances of conducting group meetings. Appreciate that the framework which supports meaningful personal connection is reproducible and transferable to any group in any faith community.

Move on to Part Two to see how the principles and methods of the group in Part One have been applied to a more contemporary venue: the book discussion group. If your book group has devolved into lifeless rounds of opinions about topics, revitalize it by adopting or adapting this process.

In Part Three, learn how the basic small group process that prioritizes connection has been adapted to address a unique opportunity: onboarding a new minister. Finally, consider how to apply the principles and techniques that enhance connection to achieve greater cohesiveness in any group, including task-oriented groups such as committees and boards. Use the included worksheet to experiment with transforming the agenda of any conventional group into one that is more effective in fostering connection.

Utilize the exhibits in the Appendix to support organizing your small groups and promoting them in a way that greatly increases the likelihood that expectations of participants can be met. Refer to the ready-to-use meeting guides while training facilitators and in conducting your own group meetings. Copy pages 89-96 in the Handouts section for your group members to use. (For copies of the exhibits and handouts in a customizable Microsoft Word document file, go to www.LifeGivingConversations.com.)

PART ONE

The Spiritual Life Dinner Group:
Breaking Bread—Serving One Another

CHAPTER 1

HOPE FOR SMALL GROUPS THAT INSPIRE CONNECTION

I still remember my uncontained joy when I walked into Mrs. Miller's first grade classroom at Old Town Elementary School in my sleepy North Carolina hometown. *At last! My tribe!* I had found what I didn't know I had been yearning for. So began my earliest outside-the-family experience of group life.

Over the years I have been a part of so many groups that I've lost count. Some were by choice. Others were due to organizational or company demands. Each was unique in its own way but all had in common one dynamic—the conscious or subconscious interplay of the needs of individuals in the group. Nowadays we call this dance "interdependence." And the dance goes on whether we are aware of it or not. Despite sharing a common faith, people in church groups often experience a dance that is less than satisfying because their group experience falls short of authentic community. That doesn't have to happen in any group.

After a corporate career, a divorce, and a geographic relocation, I found myself longing to belong. I church shopped for a while before settling on one that offered inspiring worship services and adult education classes. As the newness waned over a few months, I realized something was missing. It wasn't until a chance encounter during lunch at church conference that I got clear on what it was. After a lifetime of small groups—school, sports, corporate, vocation, family, neighborhood—I was missing small group life. Returning to my home church, I cofounded meetings of in-home dinner groups. I borrowed a model from another church and conducted the two-hour training for volunteers who stepped forward to lead the groups. The new groups were publicized. Eager congregants signed up and showed up. I was pleased when the first person who shared her gratitude with me said, "Eddie, I want to thank you for starting the dinner groups. I've been a member here for five years and I don't really know anybody."

The groups were popular. Still, I was bothered by feedback that some participants were ill at ease even after several meetings. Some people expressed their discontent, and requested that the meeting guidelines be reviewed at each meeting because their group had gotten off track. I struggled with how to more effectively train volunteer group leaders. Meanwhile, I was being pulled in other directions, and I watched the groups fade away.

A few years later, another group experience unexpectedly presented itself. A friend advised me that the Global Youth Village in Bedford, Virginia was looking for adults to work with a diverse group of teens in their summer program. I had just finished Virginia Supreme Court certification as a mediator and thought this would be a great opportunity to teach mediation. I submitted my application only to learn that my timing was off. The positions had been filled. But the camp director invited me to visit. I'm glad I did. I left the camp with a surprising new vision of small group ministry.

It was no ordinary lunch for me that day at the Global Youth Village. With the sound of the noon bell, I made my way to the camp dining hall and found a seat at one of the rectangular tables reserved for staff and volunteers. Kitchen workers brought large bowls of food and placed them on the table. What happened next is etched in my mind and embedded in my heart. Rather than the every-man-for-himself mealtime protocol that I had become accustomed to, the person to my right held a basket of bread and asked, "May I serve you?" I sat in stunned silence as I realized that everyone in the dining hall was serving and was being served in this way. I was awed by this simple, timeless gesture of connection and support. I felt a profound sense of discovery as if an ancient truth had been unearthed.

On my drive home the thought of "breaking bread—serving one another" kept coming up over and over. I knew I was called to create a small group ministry around this theme. The next day I met with my minister to share this story. In the middle of our conversation I became over-whelmed with the emotion of a life-changing insight. During lunch at the Global Youth Village, I had been given the solution to the problem of how to train group facilitators and how to support the groups in self-management from the get-go. Now I was inspired to create a new small group program that would inspire authentic community and be more robust than ever.

CHAPTER 2

IGNORE UNIVERSAL HUMAN NEEDS AT YOUR PERIL

The gist of a story from a visiting speaker stays with me after many years. At the end of World War II aid workers were appalled at the condition of orphaned infants in Romania. The infants were deplorably behind in their development. A study concluded that the reason for this tragedy was that they had not been held and nurtured. In fact, there had been very little human interaction over long periods of time. The speaker offered a surprising alternative explanation: the infants had no opportunity to give, to extend love. At first this seemed farfetched. Then I recalled how I felt recently holding a 3-month old infant. Yes, that child was contributing something to me. If it wasn't love, it must have been the next best thing.

Psychologist Marshall Rosenberg asserts that our greatest spiritual need is to contribute to the well-being of others.[1] In his book *Nonviolent Communication—A Language of Life*, Rosenberg identifies human needs that we all share.[2] The deepest of these universal needs are: to belong, to matter, to feel safe. To understand the implication regarding group life, consider what leads people to drop out of groups because these needs are not sufficiently met.

- Despite the promise of community, people feel alone in the group.
- A few people dominate the discussion and the meeting; others feel left out.
- Someone has something to share but is hesitant; they are never asked to speak.
- Vulnerable expression of a personal concern opens the floodgates to unsolicited advice, nice sounding platitudes, and other forms of well-intentioned "help."
- Participants become polarized around a topic or issue, with each side trying to convince the other that they are "right."
- Someone hijacks the group by trying to use it for therapy.
- The gathering does not begin at the scheduled time so people learn to drift in, and the start becomes ragged or is delayed even more.
- There is no scheduled ending time, or the meeting runs way past the ending time.
- Some members hang around after the meeting, unintentionally forming a subgroup that excludes the other people.

---

[1] Endnotes are given on page 98.

A small group that successfully inspires authentic community addresses three considerations. The values of the group and how it goes about achieving its goals must allow group members to:

- Feel they belong and their needs are important in the group.
- Trust they will be emotionally safe.
- Know they are contributing to the well-being of the group.

To begin a small group program without a clear way to address these universal needs invites frustration, dissatisfaction, and disconnection. Ignore these needs at your peril. When their deepest needs go unfulfilled, people eventually give up and vote with their feet—the group atrophies and dies. That doesn't have to happen.

People are yearning for the benefits of life-giving community: knowing they belong, they matter, and they contribute to the well-being of others. Paradoxically, most of us are reluctant to take responsibility for our role in shaping that community, even at church. I imagine that we are simply looking for permission to do so. I urge you to grant that permission by declaring authentic community and connection as the relational goal of every type of small group in your ministry. If you do, they will come—with enthusiasm and gratitude. People are hungry for the bread of life.

Loaves and Fishes

This is not
the age of information.

This is *not*
the age of information.

Forget the news,
and the radio,
and the blurred screen.

This is the time
of loaves
and fishes.

People are hungry
and one good word is bread
for a thousand.

—David Whyte from *The House of Belonging*
©1996 Many Rivers Press, Langley, Washington
Printed with permission from Many Rivers Press
www.davidwhyte.com

With my own goal of creating small groups that inspire connection, it was time to get practical. What would *breaking bread* in a small group look like? My first thought: in-home dinner groups meeting once a week for five weeks, the length of engagement I felt that people in my community would be willing to commit to in a new program.

What would *serving one another* look like? I had several thoughts: serving each other at least a portion of the meal, deeply listening as each person talks about what is important in his or her life, and supporting one another in prayer.

Now, the vital questions:

> How to design the group meeting so that it invites participants to step beyond everyday social interaction into enough vulnerability to make for real connection?

> How to train people who are not already highly skilled facilitators to manage a group process intended to create authentic community?

CHAPTER 3

GETTING REAL— EXPERIENCING WHAT WORKS TO SUPPORT CONNECTION

Beyond sharing a meal, I wasn't clear on what the new small group meeting should look like in practice. I wanted the elements of the meeting and how they flowed to make it easy for people to meaningfully relate to one another. Realizing that training facilitators in the classroom had its limitations, I decided to train the facilitators by *having them experience the process themselves* by participating in a group doing the process. Rather than designing the method on paper and then trying it out in a training session, I elected to combine process design and facilitator training. The plan was simple. I would enroll a half-dozen or so fellow congregants in my vision of a small group. We would meet as a dinner group, try a format and process, and experiment with various options over six or seven dinner meetings. Together we would learn what works to cultivate authentic community—and what doesn't. By trial and error, we would organically co-create a new small group method that prioritizes connection. And we would learn hands-on to facilitate a group using that process. Truly we would be "building the bridge as we were crossing the river."

The dinner groups would be rolled out to the congregation. The facilitators of the new groups would be individuals who had jointly developed the methodology. So the new groups would have facilitators who were already trained by experience. These facilitators would later support each other as they guided their own groups.

From the beginning, I publicized the name "Spiritual Life Dinner Groups" to identify the in-home groups which would use this new model for a relational small group. The response to my call for volunteers to help develop our dinner group model exceeded my expectation. I had to add a second group to accommodate all who stepped forward to be part of this experiment.

My first group meeting was unexpectedly rocky. I'm choosing to relive how painful it was so that you might understand the importance of having a plan in place. Unfortunately, I went into the meeting with only a rough outline as to what we would do, trusting that things would flow and that people would automatically open up. It didn't happen.

The dinner meeting was scheduled from 6:00 to 8:00 p.m. in a host home, with the hosts providing the main dish and others bringing side dishes. At 6:15 I found myself pacing and fidgeting in the kitchen, wondering when in the world the final three people of our group of eight would appear. *Don't they know to be here on time!* They finally arrived, and belatedly we started dinner. Soon I realized something I had known all along. There are talkers and there are folks who sit back without saying much, especially if they don't already know others in the group. Two or three people accounted for most of the dinner table conversation; others sat quietly. Not being fluent in small talk myself, self-consciously I floated out a few prompts to try to encourage fellow introverts to talk. After dessert, we adjourned to the living room. Feeling regret that I had not planned anything specific to support relaxed interactions during the meal, I was relieved to get away from the dinner table.

Debriefing brought out our shared discomfort of the dinnertime experience and birthed new tactics. One, the dinner will start at the scheduled time with places warmly held for those had not yet arrived. Two, ahead of time one person will be designated as dinnertime facilitator with the job of ensuring that everyone participates and the responsibility of selecting "table topics" or evocative icebreakers to prompt individual sharing. We concluded the evening with prayer support. More on this later.

I met with the two developmental groups over a dozen times in total. Each gathering was rich with collaboration and experimentation as we evolved the methodology for the Spiritual Life Dinner Group. Some of the things that we tried did not work for this type of group. We learned to adapt in order to include new things that supported our sense of connection. For example, everyone loved the idea of *serving one another*. But with the size of most dining room tables, that would be very crowded. So we focused on serving one another dessert at the end of the meal. Even with that simple gesture, the sacredness of the intent of serving one another was shared by all.

Even as the basic building blocks of the Spiritual Life Dinner Group emerged, it became increasingly evident that something else was needed to ensure that the groups would surpass typical expectations and would indeed inspire connection.

CHAPTER 4

GETTING PERSONAL— MEETINGS THAT MATTER

Author Brené Brown gives us two insights relevant to having meetings that matter. First, "Connection is why we're here. We are hardwired to connect with others, it's what gives purpose and meaning to our lives, and without it there is suffering." [3] Second, "Staying vulnerable is a risk we have to take if we want to experience connection." [4] It follows that in designing meetings that matter, one must successfully create and maintain an environment where people are willing to share more deeply about themselves than in typical social interactions. Preemptively setting the expectation of emotional safety and having a group process to ensure safety is the key to promoting the authenticity necessary for connection. The remainder of this chapter will detail how to develop the underlying supportive structure for safety and implement it in a way that is not burdensome to the facilitator nor to the other members in the group.

I suspect that most people in a new group hesitate to reveal what is really in their hearts because of previous experiences of discomfort in sharing something tender in a group setting. I can recall too many times witnessing someone being vulnerable, only to realize too late that unwittingly they had opened themselves up to being the recipient of all sorts of well-meaning feedback. Or, to echo the words of author Steven Covey, they exposed their soft underbelly only to have it stomped on. Many of us are not aware that our familiar reactions to someone's sharing may unintentionally communicate to that person our lack of acceptance of his or her reality rather than our compassionate understanding.

I have adapted Thomas Gordon's twelve listening roadblocks to provide examples of what *not* to do in offering support.[5] These examples are in response to a friend saying that she has become dissatisfied in her marriage and has been confiding in a male co-worker.

> **Advising**: Giving suggestions or solutions based on your knowledge and experience.
> e.g., *"I can recommend a marriage counselor who has helped several couples I personally know."*
>
> **Analyzing**: Sharing your wisdom as to why.
> e.g., *"Seeking solace outside the marriage often happens when the kids are old enough to start taking more care of themselves and we realize that we feel empty."*
>
> **Buttering Up**: Agreeing with them; approving; colluding.
> e.g., *"We all need someone to talk to. I'm glad you found someone."*
>
> **Criticizing**: Judging; letting the person know that they are in some way wrong.
> e.g., *"You've got three kids and a husband. You're not on a singles cruise. Get real."*

Distracting: Joking; changing the focus or subject.
e.g., *"That reminds me of the time I was in high school when..."*

Educating: Persuading with rational arguments; lecturing.
e.g., *"Let's think this through. The fact that you are feeling guilty shows that you haven't looked at all the issues."*

Interrogating: Using questions to guide the person to your solution to the problem.
e.g., *"What would happen if your husband found out?"*

Interpreting: Your take on the motivation behind the person's behavior.
e.g., *"I think that you are using this to avoid the problem you are having with your in-laws."*

Moralizing: Preaching; reminding the person of his or her duty or obligation.
e.g., *"You took a vow. You need to honor it."*

Ordering: Authoritatively telling the person what to do or what not to do.
e.g., *"Thank your coworker for listening but let him know that you realize that you shouldn't be looking outside of your relationship for emotional support."*

Reassuring: Helping the person to feel better.
e.g., *"Don't worry. This happened for a reason and it will all work out."*

Warning: Cautioning the person on the negative consequences if they don't change.
e.g., *"If you keep this up, it will escalate; then your marriage will fail and your kids will resent you forever."*

Do these sound familiar? They should. This is how most of us learned to respond to people in everyday life in order to influence them. And to a great extent, responses of this nature are what we have come to expect from others. But in the context of someone being vulnerable in sharing in a group, these ways of responding are problematic at best, and at their worst can quickly stimulate people to withdraw or push back. Despite the intent of the responder to be helpful, the receiver of this "support" can easily hear hidden messages: *You're at fault, you're inadequate, or your problem really isn't a problem*. The hidden messages are deep and disempowering. Hardly the stuff for building genuine relationships.

Two decades ago I enrolled in a church-sponsored creativity class. It was my first venture into the personal development genre. About the third or fourth meeting we were sitting in a circle sharing our experiences with one of the exercises in our text, Julia Cameron's *The Artist's Way*. I shared something about how the material related to a bothersome personal situation. I don't recall what I said or even what the situation was. However, I will never forget that I was immediately bombarded with advice, pithy quotations, and recommendations for books that would help me with my issue. I felt irritated, embarrassed and—worst of all—suddenly alone. That experience started me on a wide-ranging search to find more life-affirming ways for people to be with one another in small groups.

While there is often a conscious reason for responding to someone the way we do, there is also another reason—one which is not in our awareness. I'd like to pass along something I learned during a training conducted by the Academy of Coaching Excellence. While the context was one-on-one interactions, it also applies to group life. It addresses what causes us to respond to others the way we do.

Our response to someone sharing his or her distress or dreams largely stems from how we view that person. Even with the intent of encouragement and care, we are likely to respond in a disconnecting manner if we are seeing the person in any of these ways:

> They are broken and need to be fixed.
> They do not have their own answers;
> I do and it's up to me to fix them.
> I question their motivation or commitment.
> They are a drain on me. [6]

When we are willing to shift how we hold the person, we reduce the urgency to reassure and to fix, neither of which inspires connection. Spiritual support can happen when we hold the following as true for the person and for our interaction regardless of what we are observing:

> They are a hero on a hero's journey, whole and complete.
> They have their own answers.
> They have goals and dreams and want their life to make a difference.
> They are a contribution to me now.
> I interact with them in a way I want to be treated
> —with dignity and respect. [6]

I define *spiritual support* as honoring of the spirit of the person; that is, holding with care his or her need to belong, to matter, to be safe, and to make a difference. While spiritual support is important in every aspect of the dinner meeting, it is vital when people are sharing what is in their hearts. There are two essential aspects of this support. First, support for the person while they are speaking. Second, support afterwards by holding in reverence what they have expressed. We found our salon (sharing circle) to be an effective format for supporting a person in stepping far enough out of their comfort zone to share authentically. Group prayer support was a natural way to revere that expression. Neither the salon nor prayer support is successful by accident. As with every element of a Spiritual Life Dinner Group meeting, intention, unobtrusive structure, and conscious facilitation are a must.

While the format of the meeting goes a long way towards spiritual support, there is one circumstance that merits extra attention. While it happens infrequently, be prepared to handle it. I am referring to those occasional moments of intense emotion (sobbing or crying) as someone touches on something very tender for them.

What to do and what not to do with this is important as it affects every member of the group. First, what to avoid. Do not interrupt the emoting process unless it is prolonged. Do not touch or try to console or counsel the person. Do not hand tissues to the person but do have them nearby for the person to reach if they desire. When the episode subsides, do not pretend it didn't happen by moving on to the next person or the next meeting item. Rather, realize that in this moment the person feels absolutely naked before the group. A part of them that has been hidden, perhaps for decades, has just been exposed. They need the utmost compassion. At the same time, you do not want taking care of the person to occupy the remainder of the meeting.

What usually is helpful in this situation is to openly acknowledge what is happening, to let the person know they are not alone, and to give the person choice. It might go something like this (take your time):

> Let's all take a moment to honor this sharing. Take a deep breath. Raise your hand if "Susan's" sharing has been a contribution to you in some way. Raise your hand if you have felt your heart open. (Pause to allow Susan to take this in.) Susan, is there anything you would like now from any individual or from the group? (Susan may ask for someone to say how it was for them to experience her sharing or may ask for people to gather around her and place hands on her shoulders.) Susan, is there anything else you need now? (Try to accommodate.) Are you OK now with the group going on?

Should the person not be ready for the group to continue, ask if he or she would be willing to step out for a few moments with another group member. Expect that they will rejoin the group in a few minutes.

Such moments of vulnerability call for care, not caretaking; empathic connection, not words of sympathy. Don't panic. Take your time. Be with the person but don't forsake the group.

The next chapter describes the major components of a Spiritual Life Dinner Group meeting and how to effectively introduce and conduct each one in a way that honors the purpose of the group and the deepest human needs of its members. The process is applicable to similar formats such as coffee groups and dessert groups. Key elements can be integrated into task group and committee meetings to cultivate cohesiveness by allowing group members to be seen and known beyond the task at hand.

CHAPTER 5

GETTING PRACTICAL— CONDUCTING THE MEETING

Knowing each element and understanding why it is integral to the meeting is a start toward facilitating meetings that flow and feel organic. Of course, the way each element is facilitated impacts the extent to which people feel safe and know that they belong, they matter, and they are a contribution to the group. Conducting the process with ease so that the underlying structure is not a distraction to group members is the key to successful facilitation.

What follows are descriptions of the primary elements of dinner group meetings from the viewpoint of what the facilitator should do and why—important nuances that support safety, authenticity and ease of connection. (How to train facilitators is covered in Chapter 8. Materials needed are given in Exhibit L: "Checklist of Meeting Supplies.")

As you gain experience with your own groups, you'll probably make some changes in the process. Adjust the facilitator's guides accordingly.

The second meeting builds on the first. The third meeting builds on the second. Therefore, there are similar but separate facilitator guides for each of the three variants. Let's start with the first.

The FIRST Meeting

Refer to Exhibit A: "Facilitator's Guide: FIRST Spiritual Life Dinner Group Meeting" in the Appendix for a one-page summary of what to do in the initial meeting. If you do not have a co-facilitator, consider recruiting someone to support you in tracking time.

What follows is a discussion of each of the seventeen elements of the first meeting.

Arrival
Arrive about 30 minutes before the scheduled start time of the opening circle. Check in with the host or hostess to offer support in making ready the space for the meal and the space for the sharing circle (salon). Greet arriving participants, provide them name tags, introduce them to each other, and assist them in connecting with the host about what to do with the food item they brought.

Opening Circle Check-in
Convene the opening circle on time—the only way to begin on time. The primary purpose of the check-in is to allow each individual the opportunity to pause and experience brief self-awareness

so they might become more grounded and present to themselves and others. In the first meeting, take time to explain this. After brief self-connection, usually a sentence or two easily conveys the core response to the prompt: *"How I am now (in this moment)."* Mention that you are looking for a response more clear-cut than "good" or "okay." Set the tone by first sharing first. And share authentically. If you are feeling excited about this first meeting but apprehensive about facilitating, say so. To invite vulnerability, be vulnerable.

Opening Prayer
Include in prayer anyone who has not yet arrived.

Begin the Meal
Start at the scheduled time. It sounds simple enough but for those of us who value inclusion, it can be a time of great torment if everyone expected has not arrived. Say "yes" to the rest of the group and begin the meal, knowing that latecomers have been assured ahead of time they will be welcomed at the table whenever they do arrive.

Preview What to Expect During the Meal and Explain Your Role
Let the group know what's coming up: light table topics, serve one another (dessert), and short cleanup break. Give some context around each element as you mention it. For example, "We'll start to get to know one another better by taking turns responding to a few table topics." Explain that you will be participating in the sharing as well as facilitating the process.

Table Topics: Inviting Easy Self-Disclosure
Facilitated table topics during the meal provides a straightforward means of getting to know one another as well as an expectation of everyone contributing. In effect, table topics take the place of small talk which can be terribly uncomfortable for many. In the process development groups, we experimented with starting the table topics at different times during the meal. What seemed to work best was to allow a few minutes of general conversation, then to have the facilitator acknowledge that "first meetings" can sometimes feel awkward. Segue to table topics by suggesting that the group use table topics as an icebreaker and a way to hear from everyone. Announce the first topic listed in the facilitator's guide. Invite someone to volunteer to go first. Ask them to speak for about a minute to the group—not just to you. Offer guidance such as "Please give us the headlines and a summary rather than the details." The brief amount of time clues participants to get to the heart of the matter. Set a conversational tone in that what one person shares may elicit a brief response to the group from another person. Begin the second round with a different person.

Inviting a one-minute share during table topics sets the expectation of balanced participation. The reality is few people have an accurate sense of how long a minute is when they are speaking. Use a soft-tone digital timer or an hourglass minute timer to support individual awareness of the duration of one minute. Calling attention to this fact is an effective way to introduce the timer without risking mutiny. Simply run it as support, an invitation for the person sharing to start to finish what they want to share. Avoid using it in a rigid cut-off fashion. Usually people automatically adjust the duration of their remarks to about a minute, minimizing or eliminating the need to formally track time. Using a timer at the onset to have everyone experience a one minute interval sets the pace. Implementing a timer only after a long-winded share may be viewed as a "correction."

Going around the table and having participants share in the order they are seated lessens the awkward wait for someone to volunteer to speak after the previous person shares. Used repeatedly, however, this will feel stilted. After a round or two, use the volunteer or "popcorn" method but track who has shared and be prepared to coax engagement from those who have not.

Serving One Another

With the rest of the meal complete, dessert is an opportunity to experience giving and receiving by serving one another the dessert. One way is to pass the dessert tray around the table, having each person serve the one beside them. Make it a sacred moment. Let the group know that "serving one another" will continue in other parts of the meeting with deep listening during the salon and with prayer support.

Preview What to Expect after Break

The group will consider how to support one another during a period of sharing and deep listening.

Cleanup Break

After the meal is concluded, the next group activity is cleanup. Despite assurances from the host or hostess that they'll handle it, invite everyone to join in—everyone contributes. This is also a time for natural, informal socializing.

How We Want to Be with One Another: The Group Agreement

After break, the group relocates to a different area for the rest of the meeting. The space is such that all members can be accommodated with seating in a circle or at least so that they can see one another. A quiet, softly lit, distraction-free environment supports the feeling of sacred space.

The most holistic way to handle a group agreement is to begin from scratch and allocate a lot of time to surfacing everyone's needs and preferences in order to arrive at what is satisfactory to all. This approach is often used for groups intending to meet for extended periods. For short-term small group meetings this time-consuming approach is not very practical. Therefore, in this model the covenant is prewritten. It differs substantially from the typical list of "thou shalls" and "thou shall nots" because it is values-based. And the values it embodies resonate with those desiring authentic community. Even those who ordinarily dislike rules and regulations willingly embrace these guidelines that affirm: *Everyone belongs, everyone matters, everyone is a contribution.*

Distribute copies of Handout #1: "Group Agreement." Ask someone to read aloud the first item. Inquire of the group, "What would this look like in our group?" Dialogue briefly about what the item means. Usually "dos and don'ts" emerge. Ask another person to read the second item, inter-actively discuss it, and so on. Ask the group members if they are willing to give this agreement a try for their meetings. Let the them know that your role as facilitator is to be aware when the group process strays from the agreement and to request of the group that it be brought back into alignment. Be clear that you are the one responsible for supporting the group in keeping its agreement; otherwise, someone might take it upon themselves to be the "enforcer" and make it about the person rather than the process. Should you be concerned that the buy-in is not sincere or that one or more participants are resistant, go further. Ask each person to respond briefly to two questions:

> *Which parts of the agreement will be easy for you to keep?*
> *Which parts of the agreement might not be so easy for you to keep?*

Without making anyone wrong, acknowledge what is said. Ask for willingness to give the agreement a try. Remind the group that there will be a round of feedback at the end of the meeting, an opportunity for everyone to share leadership.

At each meeting, place a copy of the Group Agreement nearby, say on a coffee table in the center of the circle, so that it is visible. If your verbal direction to realign the group process with the agreement isn't effective, pause the meeting and revisit the agreement with the group.

With the agreement in place, the way is clear for the most intimate part of the meeting, the salon or sharing circle. While the time for sharing is relatively brief, in our groups people seemed to naturally surface what they really cared about, what they valued, what mattered to them. And like nothing else I've experienced in small groups, this authenticity promotes connection.

The Salon: A Container for Genuine Sharing and Deep Listening

My encounter with a salon during a men's group retreat was the spark that inspired me to see it as a possibility for the Spiritual Life Dinner Group. I had found that the simple, safe structure of the salon invited much deeper sharing and greater sense of connection than had been the norm. Lucky for me, the facilitator was a member of our first process development group and happily agreed to guide us. With that experience, we adopted the salon as an essential element of the Spiritual Life Dinner Group to promote meaningful connection. The salon is an opportunity for each person to share something that is important to them and to be heard by each one in the group. Our salon may differ substantially from others familiar to you. I'll describe how to gracefully set the stage for the salon and how to conduct it so that it feels as sacred as it truly is.

After the group agreement segment, explain the purpose of the salon and how it will be conducted. For example:

> *The purpose of our salon is to create the space for each of us to touch on and share what is true for us—what really matters—while having the support of the group in the form of the deep listening. So that each of us may feel heard in the next half hour, we have two simple guidelines to support respect and safety.*
>
> *When sharing: Speak from your heart. Be spontaneous. Speak to the entire group, not just to any one person. Speak about yourself and your experience, not about someone else or what someone in the circle has shared.*

When listening: Be present to the speaker, listening with your ears and with your heart. When you become aware that you are not present, simply bring your attention back to the speaker. Listen only—no feedback, no crosstalk.

How we are choosing to be with one another now is radical departure from our everyday communication patterns so it's easy to drift away from the guidelines. Should that happen, are you willing to hear a gentle reminder from me about our guidelines? (Visually check with each person or ask.)

Finally, are you willing to hold in confidence everything shared here? (Visually check with each person or ask.)

Often we will begin the salon with a short reading before I pose a question or announce a topic. After a moment for reflection, I'll invite someone to share first, then we'll go around the circle.

The first round will be two minutes for each of us and the second round will be one minute. Each of us will have the same amount of time and if we complete what we have to say before time is up, the group will hold silence for us. Often when we reflect in silence, we will find that we have more to say. When you hear the soft tone of the timer, that's an invitation to start to complete your sharing.

Of course, as the facilitator you will want to convey your understanding of the salon in your own words, pausing for dialogue with the participants.

Refer to Exhibit B: "'On Listening' Article." This is the reading for this first salon. Have each participant read aloud a section of the article. Then announce the salon topic for the first round: *"A time I felt heard and understood."* Pause briefly to allow time for reflection. Then call for a volunteer to be the first to share. When that person finishes, the group then is present to another person as they share. With this salon process there is no feedback or verbal appreciation after each person speaks; there is simply quiet reverence as the group prepares to hear the next person. It is usually more efficient to just go around the circle rather than wait for the next speaker to volunteer. If someone isn't ready to speak they "pass" and are invited later. After everyone (including yourself as the facilitator) shares, announce the topic for the second round: *"My experience of sharing in the first round; and my experience of being the listener."* Invite a different volunteer to go first.

In earlier groups, we used the "talking stick" method of conducting the salon with the suggestion to "talk for a few minutes" on the topic, and without any tracking of time. Some people spoke at length with great detail. Others spoke a few sentences and then quickly passed the stick to the next person. The amount of time that participants spoke to the group varied from a fraction of a minute to five minutes or so. The palpable energetic quality in the room varied greatly from speaker to speaker. After we adopted the same-amount-of-time-for-each-person method, the depth of individual sharing increased markedly as did the sense of connection with the speaker.

The allotted time for the salon is thirty minutes. Allowing for time to review the salon guidelines and to introduce the salon topic to the group, each participant (for a group of eight) would have an average of just over three minutes total. At first glance, three minutes sharing per person doesn't seem like enough time to be meaningful. However, sharing during the table topics paves the way for the salon. Further, as people realize that their needs for safety and respect are being honored, they become more at ease in sharing something personal and significant.

At the start of each salon round, announce the amount of time each person has for sharing and provide a means to keep track of the time. *Self-monitoring of time isn't effective* as evidenced in a meeting of one training group where the salon ran some twenty minutes over. Someone must track time and do so unobtrusively. There are several ways to track the time without it being a distraction.

An hourglass minute timer is silent but requires that the timekeeper briefly look at it to see when the time increment is up. A slight raising of the hand signals the speaker to begin completing his or her remarks. A soft audible signal works well as it serves to support the person speaking in closing while signaling a transition to the next person. Once the audible timer is set, the timekeeper is free to be fully present to the person sharing. Something that works very well is a smart phone that has a digital timer with a soft harp or chime tone. You can silence the tone or set the volume so low that it's barely audible and use a hand signal instead. Do not use a loud tone or a racy, attention-getting ringtone. If you or an assistant are going to use a digital timer, experiment with it before the meeting. Fussing with the timer during the meeting will make it object of attention. At that point there is nothing one can do to keep the meeting from feeling regimented. When employed with practiced care, the soft-tone digital timer is not a distraction but rather a gentle support for the group process. (Some kitchen timers beep with every push of a reset button and many timers sound an intrusive buzzer or alarm—do not use these.)

As silence is held after someone ceases to speak but with time remaining, they usually will resume sharing. Inevitably they will be getting to the heart of what is important to them. This is the primary reason to avoid using the "talking stick" method. When people complete verbalizing a thought without another clear one immediately following, they tend to pass the stick, resulting in a missed opportunity to reflect and go deeper. On the other hand, when participants know they have time remaining, most will reflect and offer even greater clarity about what is most important to them.

It is common to feel uncomfortable with silence while being the focus of attention. Built into the salon for the first meeting is a round to allow everyone to express how they experienced being the speaker as well as being the listener. If they paused while sharing, people will usually talk about how it was for them to experience being held in silence. From the role as listeners, people would usually tell how it was for them to hold silence for those who paused their sharing to collect their thoughts. Any initial discomfort associated with sharing or deep listening in the salon is usually transmuted into a sense of acceptance, inclusion, and care.

Prayer Support

For many, giving and receiving prayer support will be the most fulfilling aspect of this small group experience. *From participants in the first round of our Spiritual Life Dinner Groups:*

> "Prayer works. We could feel the team prayer working all week."

> "The group met my need for support with life issues –by prayer and love."

> "It was powerful to share prayer requests and then hold each member's request during the week."

During the sign-up period for the groups, the most frequently expressed reservation about joining a group will likely be concerns around prayer support. "I've never prayed out loud for anyone." "I'm not good at prayer in public." "I'm afraid to pray in a group." "I can't seem to find the right words—I'll be embarrassed."

In many churches, it is not unusual that when a meeting is opened up for prayer requests, only a few people *make a request for themselves.* Most often their request is on behalf of a relative or friend or a population that is suffering. For many, the dinner group could be the first time that they have publicly voiced their own personal prayer need. The increased sense of intimacy and connection arising from a personal request to be supported in prayer quickly dissolves any concern of vulnerability. When setting up the prayer support portion of the meeting, take extra care to invite participants to make their prayer request for themselves.

It is important that the prayer support be inclusive and participatory rather than just having one person designated to say a prayer for each individual or collectively for everyone. A sense of interdependence in prayer support helps to create authentic community. What is needed is a simple, easy method where everyone participates equally and no one is put on the spot to perform. A spontaneous expression as opposed to a rote prayer inspires connection as well. An easy-to-learn three-part affirmative prayer method proved successful in our first process development groups.[7] We've used it successfully in all of the subsequent rounds of dinner groups.

In teaching prayer support, putting everyone at ease is crucial. One way to do so is to share how it was for you in your training group when you learned this form of prayer support. Using a worksheet makes it easy for people to learn the method at the first meeting. Before handing out the worksheet, briefly dialogue with participants about their name for God and where God is, volunteering your responses. Emphasize that this is an opportunity to ask for prayer for themselves rather than for another person. Distribute copies of Handout #2: "Affirmative Prayer Worksheet." Walk through a few of the examples, having participants read them aloud in the three parts: my name for God, where God is, the good I want to affirm *for myself.* Ask participants to reflect on their prayer need and to write it down in the blank space at the end of the table on the worksheet.

In the prayer circle, invite participants one at a time to say (or read) their three-part prayer request. Others hold that request in silent prayer briefly (say, fifteen seconds), then when prompted, together say "Amen" or "And so it is" or another appropriate close. The prayer support continues until the next meeting by having everyone create a list of the all the requests to hold in prayer daily. We did that by writing down the essence of each request. The essence is often expressed in a one word in response to the question "And what would that bring you?" Typical responses are: "peace," "freedom," "joy," "health." Next to each person's name on an index card, write their request or the essence of their request. Refer to the card during daily prayer until the next meeting. Of course, a smart phone or tablet can be used as well.

The three-part prayer method described here is especially empowering because each person crafts his or her own request and gives it his or her voice. If this method does not resonate with you or your tradition, simply go with what is familiar or comfortable. To the extent possible, structure it so it is easy, is a group process, includes each person's personal prayer request *for themselves,* and does not put people on the spot to perform.

Once they experience the prayer support, group members will understand why this group process explicitly excludes familiar interventions such as advice-giving, reassuring, and educating. Prayer supersedes any personal intervention from fellow group members. During the salon at the next group meeting, participants will have the opportunity to speak about how it was for them to pray daily for members of the group.

People enjoy supporting one another in prayer especially when all participate equally as partners in community. Daily prayer support gives everyone the opportunity to contribute, to make a difference for others.

Arrangements for the Next Meeting
Immediately after prayer support, the group decides on arrangements for the next meeting. Get commitments for the upcoming meeting at the close of the current meeting. Subsequently confirm assignments and responsibilities (as well as host home address and phone number if the next meeting is in a different home) to all well in advance of the next meeting.

Feedback Round on this Meeting
With almost all aspects of the meeting predetermined, affording group members the opportunity to give feedback can only enhance their sense of belonging and mattering. Request that they express what specifically in the meeting worked well for them and what might make the meeting more fulfilling. Weigh this input in preparing for the next meeting.

Closing Circle
Invite someone to offer a short prayer honoring the time together.

End as a Group
Finally, say farewells and have guests *leave the host home on time and as a group.* Do not permit

anyone to stay around after the close even to help tidy up as this can be burdensome to the hosts and establishes a *de facto* subgroup which is not inclusive. When the meeting is over, it's over.

Daily Prayer Support for the Week
Everyone leaves with a card noting the prayer requests for others in the group and with the commitment to support one another in prayer daily.

The SECOND Meeting

Refer to Exhibit C: "Facilitator's Guide: SECOND Spiritual Life Dinner Group Meeting" for a one-page summary of what to do in the second meeting. Most of the elements are identical to the first meeting, and will not be discussed again here. Major elements of the second meeting are listed as follows along with key differences from the first meeting noted.

Arrival

Opening Circle Check-in

Opening Prayer

Begin the Meal

Preview What to Expect During the Meal

Table Topics

> Different preselected evocative icebreakers are given in the meeting guide (Exhibit C)

Serving One Another

Preview What to Expect after Break

Cleanup Break

How We Want to Be with One Another: The Group Agreement
Revisit the Group Agreement by having it read aloud in sections. If there were major excursions from the guidelines during the first meeting, take time to dialogue about each item. Ask the group members for their willingness to honor the agreement.

The Salon: A Container for Genuine Sharing and Deep Listening
Two new preselected salon topics are given in the guide (Exhibit C). Note also that the allotted times are different by design. In this salon the first round is one minute and the second round is three minutes. The first topic, *"Praying daily for those in this group,"* gives everyone the opportunity to say something about their experience in contributing prayer support on a daily basis. The second topic is more open-ended. *"Something that is going well in my life; something that is a challenge,"* invites group members to speak about something important to them. People are more likely to connect on the basis of what really matters rather than the particulars of their stories. The suggested time constraint supports people in stepping around their stories and into the heart of what matters.

Prayer Support

Arrangements for the Next Meeting

Closing Circle

End as a Group

Daily Prayer Support for the Week

The THIRD Meeting

Refer to Exhibit D: "Facilitator's Guide: THIRD Spiritual Life Dinner Group Meeting" for a one-page summary of what to do in the third meeting and meetings thereafter. Major elements of these meetings are as follows, with differences from the second meeting noted.

Arrival

Opening Circle Check-in

Opening Prayer

Begin the Meal
Choose up to three new table topics from the list included in Exhibit E: "Table Topics (Evocative Icebreakers)."

Serving One Another

Cleanup Break

How We Want to Be with One Another
Usually by the third meeting the Group Agreement has been followed sufficiently that it is not necessary to review it. Keeping a copy where it is visible nearby is a reminder.

The Salon
In this salon the first round topic is "*What I am noticing about myself lately.*" The second round topic is chosen from the list in Exhibit F: "Salon Topics (Deep Sharing)." In the final meeting of the group, consider including a salon round on *"What being in this group has meant to me."*

Prayer Support

Arrangements for the Next Meeting

Closing Circle

End as a Group

Daily Prayer Support for the Week

The FOURTH and FIFTH Meetings

For these meetings, follow the guide for the third meeting.

CHAPTER 6

THE ROLE OF STRUCTURE

Some types of groups rely on skilled facilitators to evaluate what is happening in the moment and then decide on how to intervene. This small group process relies heavily on its organizing principle: *Everyone belongs, everyone matters, everyone is a contribution.* The method resulting from honoring these values paves the way for a fulfilling experience for all group members. However, how the group looks and feels to participants will depend on how well the facilitator knows the process and in what way he or she implements it. The more the facilitator makes the meeting about authentically connecting with those in the group, the more group members will be inclined to respond in kind. So the challenge to the facilitator is to integrate his or her training and the supporting exhibits in the Appendix and Handouts sections to guide each meeting in such a manner that "structure" seems almost invisible to group members. Structure is not something that the facilitator imposes on the group. Rather, structure is what that upholds the facilitator as the facilitator upholds the highest aspirations of the group.

In preparing for a recent presentation on small group ministry to a regional church conference, I was cautioned by organizers that one relevant demographic (popularly known as cultural creatives) did not like structure. While that may be true, I have yet to encounter a person who does not need to belong and know that they matter. In order for the group process be in service of these universal human needs, as facilitator you simply must have structure *for yourself.* Failing to know and integrate the group process method with your way of being with the group will result in a meeting that feels either chaotic or regimented, depending on whether there is largely an absence of structure or an attempt to figure out the structure while the meeting is in progress.

In considering structure, we usually think of the meeting format perhaps along with any handout materials and so forth. There is another aspect of structure that is important to the success of the Spiritual Life Dinner Group. It is the conscious objective in everything that precedes the meeting to communicate the purpose of the groups, what the participant can expect from the group and what the group expects from the participant. It's about managing expectations by proactively addressing cares and concerns. Because emails, websites and handouts often go unread, personal contact is vital in managing expectations. Other than face-to-face interaction, the old-fashion phone conversation is the best way to ensure mutual understanding about the groups. Here's what to do, even if you registered participants in person:

- Make welcome calls to group members within a few days of sign up
- Confirm their understanding of the purpose of the groups
- Confirm their understanding of the guidelines and Group Agreement
- Let them know what to do should they arrive after the start time

- Confirm their commitment to faithful attendance
- Ask about any concerns they may have
- Verify host home / directions / phone number; give your phone number
- Assign or confirm food item to be brought (food to be prepared in advance)
- Inquire about special dietary needs, allergies, etc.
- Request to be notified if the person is unable to attend

With face-to-face or phone interaction with each group member before the first meeting, the facilitator will have begun the connection with all participants and each participant will have started to relate to at least one other member of the group. Without this vital pre-meeting dialogue, the first meeting will feel stiff—a natural result of uncertainty with not having a shared under-standing as to purpose, process, and expectations. Inspire connection by modeling behavior that reflects what you want for your group. To get connection, be connecting.

Some aspects of structure that are seen and known by group members make facilitating easier. For example, suppose that there is no group agreement regarding respectful listening. At the meeting someone interrupts another person. You notice, hoping that it will not happen again. But it does. You realize that if you do not intervene, the meeting will rapidly lose focus and deteriorate as more people feel increasing discomfort. Now you face a dilemma: how to elevate the group process to the desired standard of respectful listening without making wrong the person who did not adhere to the unspoken standard. It is much more effective to be upfront and transparent about well-known potential problems in groups than to try to issue a "correction" in the middle of a meeting. With the Group Agreement included early in the publicity about upcoming groups, reviewed with each participant during personal contact in advance of the first meeting and sanctioned by participants during the first meeting, not only have you been given permission to uphold the agreement, it is expected of you. If someone interrupts during the meeting, it is easy to simply call for coming back into alignment with the Group Agreement.

CHAPTER 7

THE ROLE OF THE FACILITATOR

Fa·cil·i·tate means to make easier; help bring about (Merriam-Webster)

The role of the facilitator is to help bring about the intended outcome of the group—authentic community and connection—and to make it easy for group members to live into that intention. Simply put, the facilitator guides the process of being together.

Many groups depend on a strong group leader to direct discussion to a conclusion or a teacher to share his or her knowledge. In the Spiritual Life Dinner Group, the facilitator leads himself or herself in maintaining a high consciousness that, in turn, inspires group members to relax and to share what matters to them on a deeper level (as opposed to just offering an opinion about a topic). The result is the treasured satisfaction of authentic community. The facilitator is not a counselor, advisor, spiritual director, problem solver, coach, or advocate.

In a Spiritual Life Dinner Group, the facilitator:

- Guides members to a shared understanding of how they want to be with one another

- Participates as a sharing member of the group

- Models authenticity and relational presence (rather than task orientation)

- Manages the group process

- Notices when the group process is drifting from the Group Agreement, and without making anyone wrong, brings that to the attention of the group and invites a shift

- Inspires engagement and balanced participation

- Provides materials for each meeting

> ### Facilitator's Mantra
>
> It's not about me.
> I'm not the expert.
> The answer is in the room.

CHAPTER 8

HOW TO TRAIN AND SUPPORT FACILITATORS

Even without being a highly experienced facilitator, almost anyone who relates well to people and is passionate about creating authentic community can successfully lead a dinner group. The person must be willing to invest the time to learn and practice (in group) the methodology and to embody the principles presented in this book. This assumes, of course, that the appropriate groundwork has been laid to achieve a shared understanding with participants as to the purpose of the groups and how group members agree to be with one another.

In preparing to guide their dinner groups, candidate facilitators will need to do more than just read this book. They need to learn the group process by living it and by practicing its components. Therefore, the facilitator training is a co-learning practice group, and at the same time it is an authentic group with interactions, sharing, and prayer support just as if it were a "real" group. It is important that while the candidate facilitators are practicing the parts of the process, they also live the process. Otherwise, they will not understand the experience they will be attempting to facilitate for their groups once they start meeting. Living the training makes it organic rather than a paint-by-numbers scheme.

Recruiting

For each practice group, enroll six to eight people who support purpose of the Spiritual Life Dinner Group, are interested in facilitating a group, and are willing to learn and contribute to others in a multi-week learning group.

In recruiting people for the facilitator training, I held question and answer sessions. A few candidates voiced objections of having to go through the learning group process to become a group facilitator because they've "been working with groups for years." Realizing that my vision for this small group ministry was specific and unlike any I had experienced, I resisted the temptation to give in. I insisted that all candidate facilitators participate in the learning group before facilitating their own group. Some people pushed back. I was resolute. Some would-be facilitators chose to not participate. I mention this because you will likely be challenged when you make participation in your training group a requirement for those who want to facilitate a group in your ministry. Be clear on this yourself. What comes up for you as you consider being firm on this requirement? Work through this, with help if necessary, so that you are prepared to address the issue when it arises.

Interview in person everyone who signs up to express interest in becoming a facilitator. Why? There are three considerations. First, the interview is natural way to start establishing the personal relationship or to extend an existing personal relationship in the context of training and service. Second, the interview should enable you to readily discern whether the candidate facilitator is in alignment with the vision and purpose of the groups. If any candidate facilitator in your training group is not truly on board with the vision and mission for the groups or is attached to his or her way of leading a group, it will eventually surface within the training group as conflict or in that person's group as a disconnect between what participants expect and what is being offered. Third, the face-to-face interview allows you and the candidate to discuss whether the candidate is clear at this time to assume the added responsibility of facilitating a group. Major life events such as martial separation or divorce may be barriers. There is no need to overstep your pay grade here; if in doubt, refer the candidate to the senior minister or appropriate clergy for further consideration.

Practice Group: First Meeting

Assuming that no one is experienced in the Spiritual Life Dinner Group methodology, the candidate facilitators will together learn and practice the process in about four or more meetings. Someone will likely emerge as the champion of this new type of group or perhaps as the savviest with respect to group process in general. While it would be natural for this person to take (or be given) the lead, consider the advantage of having co-leaders. With only one leader, key learning may be overlooked while attention is on the steps in the process. The remainder of this section assumes co-leaders.

In preparation for the first practice group meeting, all involved read and study Part One of this book in order to start developing an understanding of why each element of the process is like it is. Using Exhibit A: "Facilitator's Guide: FIRST Spiritual Life Dinner Group Meeting," the co-leaders act as facilitators of first practice group meeting, allocating the various sections of the meeting between them. Roughly, the meeting can be divided into sections as follows:

(a) Opening
(b) Meal / Break
(c) Group Agreement
(d) Salon
(e) Prayer Support
(f) Closing

Because this is a learning group and not a "this is how to do it" training by an expert, capturing the learning must be intentional and collaborative. Here is one way to facilitate group learning in the absence of an expert. After one co-leader completes a section of the meeting, the other "feedback" co-leader asks three questions, pausing after each for the response:

• *What were you trying to accomplish in this part of the meeting?*
• *What did you do well?*
• *What would you do differently?*

After these responses, the feedback co-leader asks the others to summarize succinctly the learning from this experience and to offer suggestions for improvement. This sorting out of what works and what doesn't work so well clarifies and embeds the methodology in a way unachievable by written procedure, no matter how through. That said, avoid debate. Simply record suggestions and address them at the end of the practice meeting.

With completion of all the meeting elements listed in the guide, debrief the overall process and discuss which of the suggestions to incorporate. With the conclusion of this practice portion of the meeting, assign people sections to facilitate in the next practice meeting.

Practice Group: Meetings 2-4

Use Exhibit A: "Facilitator's Guide: FIRST Spiritual Life Dinner Group Meeting" for each of the practice group meetings as it contains all of the major elements. However, in the second practice meeting use table topics and salon topics listed for Exhibit C: "Facilitator's Guide: SECOND Spiritual Life Dinner Group Meeting." For the third and fourth practice meetings, use topics as noted in Exhibit D: "Facilitator's Guide: THIRD Spiritual Life Dinner Group Meeting."

It is necessary that each person practice and receive feedback on setting up the table topics, group agreement, salon and prayer support. These are the crucial constituents that strongly influence the quality of the group experience. Allow time after for individual practice at the end of the fourth practice group, or schedule another meeting dedicated to everyone practicing how to introduce these elements in a meeting. It's not about the facilitator following a script or agenda, but rather about maintaining relational presence. Guide the group through the parts of the meeting while coming from the awareness that everyone belongs, everyone matters, and everyone is making a difference.

The Facilitator in Action in Practice Group Meetings

The practice group is more than getting through the agenda. With four or so meetings, most likely many of the challenges in real groups will surface. These are opportunities for facilitator to practice handling those situations. Debriefing how these situations were dealt with will increase the learning for all.

For example, say the schedule calls for the meeting to begin at 6 p.m., and it is 6:05. Two of the expected eight people are not there. As facilitator, your choice is to wait on the two to arrive (perhaps tugging at your value of inclusion) or to begin the meeting (thus honoring those present). You may feel torn. Here's one way to begin on time while also including late-comers. You might say, "I notice that it is a few minutes after six. Let's include Robert and Monique in our opening prayer and hold a space for them at the table as we begin."

Here's an example of what could happen during a salon. A participant takes his turn and addresses the person who just shared, commenting on what was said. Interrupting, you might say "Let's bring our process into alignment with our agreement which call for speaking to the entire group and sharing about ourselves and our own experience." Everyone in the group knows that as the facilitator you were given permission ahead of time to offer this kind of clarity. They will be glad that you are honoring for their needs for predictability, safety, and respect.

CHAPTER 9

HOW TO ORGANIZE AND PROMOTE
SPIRITUAL LIFE DINNER GROUPS

The steps and timetable listed in the Appendix, Exhibit G: "Steps to Self-Sustaining Groups," are formulated for the leader or team initiating the Spiritual Life Dinner Group (dinner, lunch or coffee meetings) within the small group ministry. A brief explanation of each step is given as follows.

Step 1. Cast an Inspiring Vision and Compelling Mission for Your Small Groups

> *If you want to build a ship, don't drum up people to collect wood and don't assign them tasks and work, but rather teach them to long for the endless immensity of the sea.* — Antoine de Saint-Exupery

Vision: What will your religious or spiritual community look like and feel like after your small groups are implemented and successful? What is new, different? How are individuals and the church or spiritual center benefitting?

Mission: How is this vision to be accomplished; by what means?

Soul: The often overlooked organizing principle or core values upon which the program is founded is the soul of small group ministry. To understand the soul of your program, ask, "What do we stand for?" *Everyone belongs, everyone matters, everyone is a contribution* is the soul of Spiritual Life Dinner Groups as well as the groups discussed in Parts Two and Three of this book.

If a team is initiating the program, team members would meet to create the vision some four and one-half months ahead of the anticipated first small group meetings for congregants.

a. Enroll stakeholders in the idea of starting Spiritual Life Dinner Groups

If you are not the decision maker, you will want to enroll the appropriate person(s) or committee to gain support for the initiative. Be prepared to hear something like this: *We tried small groups in the past. They just didn't work.* Don't be surprised by this response. Because there are many perspectives on what small group ministry is, *enroll stakeholders in your specific vision and mission* rather than trying to sell a generic small group ministry. This is best done face-to-face rather than by email or filling out forms. Remember, many people have had less than wonderful experiences in small groups. Your groups will be different because of your commitment to inspiring connection, your understanding that without vulnerability there is no connection, your experience in living the group process in the practice group (along with candidate facilitators), and your follow-through with facilitator support.

b. Form a coordinating team

Ideally, the team would consist of the minister or associate minister along with several people who believe in the initiative. Look for those who are committed to participating in the co-learning practice group and afterwards being available to facilitate a group in the first round of meetings.

c. Choose a name or theme

A name for your groups or small group ministry that embodies the essence of your vision conveys a constant message which invites people into alignment with that vision.

d. Create or adopt a logo that reflects your theme

Graphics or a logo that reflect your theme anchors your written message. Consistently used on flyers, handout materials, and the web, such a logo instantly informs people that the material they are about to see relates to the small groups. If you lift a logo from the internet, you may need to get permission to use it.

Step 2. Decide on a Launch Date for the Groups and the Number of Weeks to Meet

My experience with the Spiritual Life Dinner Group model has been with groups that met from five to eight weeks. Especially for the first round of groups in your church, consider a shorter rather than longer time frame. It seems that about five meetings are sufficient for people in the groups to feel genuinely connected. Keep in mind that the facilitators will have several weeks of practice meetings just prior to starting their own groups, a significant time commitment. What to do after the prescribed period of meetings is over is addressed in Chapter 10.

Step 3. Release an Initial (General) Announcement

Let people know what's coming—the purpose and general time frame of the groups. Usually it is not known with certainty at this time who the facilitators will be nor exactly what days of the week or times groups will be available. See Exhibit H: "Sample Announcement for Spiritual Life Dinner Groups" for an example of a general announcement.

Step 4. Call for group facilitators

The call for facilitators can be included in the initial announcement about the groups. Be up front about your expectations. Use whatever is customary in your community to obtain contact infor-mation. See sample in Exhibit I: "Sample Facilitator Interview Sign-up Form."

Step 5. Interview Candidate Facilitators

A personal interview is a must, even if it's fifteen minutes. It starts the relationship and provides an opportunity for the candidate and the interviewer to discern whether this type of group methodology will work for the candidate. (See Exhibit J: "Facilitator Interview Guide.") Prior to the interview, be sure to provide the candidate the "Group Agreement," "General Guidelines for Spiritual Life Dinner Groups," and "Frequently Asked Questions: Spiritual Life Dinner Groups," (Handouts #1, #3, and #4 in the Handouts section following the Appendix). Request that they review these materials before the interview.

Step 6. Train Facilitators
See Chapter 8.

Step 7. Release Detailed Publicity for Open Sign Up
With firm commitments from qualified facilitators, the calendar can be set and publicized. Wanting to honor the commitment made by my facilitators, I simply had them choose days and times for their own groups to meet. Our poster was designed to pique interest and inform congregants as to "who, what, when, where." See Exhibit K: "Sample Meeting Venues Poster." This was added to our website along with specific dates and times for each group.

So that participants might know what they are signing up for, be sure to publicize the "Group Agreement," "General Guidelines for Spiritual Life Dinner Groups," and "Frequently Asked Questions." Make these readily available in handout packets so that people will have the opportunity to consider group norms that may differ markedly from what they may be accustomed to.

Step 8. Conduct Q&A Sessions for People Interested in Joining a Group
Even with all the publicity, people may not have a clear understanding about what they are committing to. You will want that understanding to happen in order to minimize no-shows and dropouts. *Don't assume that people have obtained and read the written materials.* Hold sessions between or after regular services or initiate community gatherings for a few weeks to engage people direct. Provide a brief overview of the groups. Emphasize how each participant is key to the success of the group and that in registering for a group each is committing to be faithful in attendance by making the groups a priority. These are not drop-in groups. Educate people on this point.

Step 9. Sign Up Participants for New Groups
For in-person registration, recruit the group facilitators to staff the sign-up table. Use a form such as Exhibit M: "Participant Sign-up Sheet" to capture contact information. Make sure that each person registering has a copy of the "Group Agreement," "General Guidelines for Spiritual Life Dinner Groups" as well as "Frequently Asked Questions." Depending on the precedent for sign ups, allow up to three weeks for participants to register.

Step 10. Model Personal Contact
Be diligent in maintaining contact with the facilitators as they enroll participants and prepare to begin their groups meetings. The facilitators will make or break the groups. Especially support them in doing the one thing most vital to a successful first group meeting: connecting with each group member prior to that first meeting by face-to-face or phone conversation. Sure, the information can be conveyed by email, text or voice message. But as David Whyte writes, this is not the age of information—people are hungry for one good word. The personal conversation ensures that when the group meets, every person will be acquainted with at least one other in the group. The more the personal contact by the facilitator before the first meeting, the less stiff that first meeting will feel. The personal conversation is by far the best way to minimize the likelihood of misunderstandings which result in no-shows and dropouts.

Step 11. Start the Group Meetings

About 5-7 days before the start of meetings, find out from the facilitators whether the number of people in their group has changed. If a group is short members, try to fill spaces by having the facilitator, the other group members or yourself recruit replacements. Make sure anyone so joining the group is truly interested, not just extending a favor.

Step 12. Support Facilitators after Their First Group Meetings

Maintain contact with facilitators after the groups start meeting to address their cares and concerns. One of the easiest ways to support facilitators is to schedule a telephone conference after the first week of meetings. Even with a dozen facilitators on the call, it takes less than an hour to celebrate and learn from one another. Here are three questions I typically ask each facilitator on the call to respond to in under two minutes. *What did you most enjoy about the group? What did you do well? What might you do differently next time?*

In this or any other debriefing, avoid getting into details should a facilitator have a challenge with an individual participant. Generalize the situation and coach about the process. Offer one-on-one support off-line.

Step 13. Capture Feedback and Testimonials

To get the most candid feedback from group members, use an internet survey. Another option is to use a feedback form distributed by hard copy or email. See Handout #5: "Participant Feedback Form" for an example.

Step 14. Integrate Learning into Plans for the Next Round

Within a few weeks of the last meeting, arrange a luncheon or dinner with your facilitators to celebrate. Enjoy sharing peak experiences and ideas for improvements.

Step 15. Obtain Recommendations for Facilitators of Future Groups

Canvass facilitators for their input on who in their group would likely enjoy facilitating a future group. With enough recommendations for people already experienced in how the group method-ology supports forming authentic community, the stage is set for a new round of groups. Even if all candidate facilitators for the second round were participants in a first round group, conduct at least a few practice Spiritual Life Group Dinner meetings to train them in the nuances of each component of the meeting by having them facilitate parts of the practice group. In the practice group, the facilitators for the next round of groups get to know and support one another as well as integrate learning from the first round.

CHAPTER 10

SOLUTIONS TO ISSUES THAT MAY ARISE
IN SETTING UP THE GROUPS

The number of persons in a group

A group of six seems to be the minimum for an effective group. With a group of ten or more, each person has much less time to speak and much more time to spend listening. Generally, as the number of people in a group increases, the ease of being vulnerable decreases. Eight seems to be an ideal size which can also be comfortably accommodated in most homes. All announcements about sign ups should carry the caveat on group size: the minimum (six) and the maximum (eight). Our sign-up sheets had space for eight, including the facilitator, so that later one more participant could be added if absolutely necessary (i.e., if there were no other group for them). I trusted divine order around this. It always worked out.

Securing the commitment of participants who sign up to show up

Imagine that eight people sign up for a particular group and at the first meeting, and four show up. Bummer. To lessen the odds of having this unfortunate circumstance, you must be proactive and persistent. Written caveats in the promotional materials are a given, but don't rely on them exclusively. Always have someone, preferably the facilitators themselves, at the sign-up table who will educate potential participants on how the group process is designed for a certain number of participants and that their commitment to be faithful in attendance is needed. Even with a verbal commitment from registrants, each facilitator should personally contact those registered to reconfirm their attendance. Have these contacts done before the end of the sign-up period so that you will know which groups have openings for additional members.

The number of groups for the initial round

For the first round of groups, the number of groups can be no greater than the number of people in the training group. Why? Because to qualify to facilitate a group, one must have had the group experience themselves and the hands-on practice of conducting the elements of the process in the practice group. An initial core of eight facilitators would suggest that up to eight groups could be formed, fewer if some groups have co-facilitators. To have more groups available, conduct additional training groups. For larger congregations consider a pilot program where some of the initial eight people graduating from the practice group form new practice groups for new trainees.

When the number of available facilitators exceeds the number of viable groups

Matching the number of facilitators to the demand for groups is inexact, mainly because one does not know how many people will be registering for the round of groups. Further, some of those completing the training may decide not to take on a group themselves as facilitator. Before the facilitator training begins, let candidates know it is possible that the group they will offer may not have enough people registering to be viable. If the group doesn't form, those affected will be offered options of joining another group.

There seems to be too many groups offered at the same time
Say there are three facilitators who want Wednesday night groups. Depending of the size of the church, one might wonder if all three groups will have the minimum number of people. If none is willing to switch to a different meeting day, meet with the three facilitators to draw straws. Place two sign-up sheets out and hold the third back pending the first two groups filling up. If feasible, arrange co-facilitating ahead of time as a contingency should the third group not be viable.

Where to find host homes
If the facilitator wants to be a host home and has suitable accommodations, then list them as the host home on the sign-up sheet. Not all facilitators care to host the meetings in their home. Some may not have the facilities needed. On these sign-up sheets include a column "Can you be a host home?" I've yet to have the situation where there wasn't at least one person in the group who could host. Be sure that the home meets these parameters: quiet, smoke-free, accessible, available parking or public transportation, and can comfortably accommodate the number of people designated for a meal and a sharing circle. Some people are allergic to pets so include any pet information on the sign-up sheet so that people can have choice. Be aware that pets can be a major distraction. Do not have pets in the meeting areas.

One host home vs. rotating the meetings
I left it up to the facilitators whether their group would always meet in the same host home or would rotate among members of the group who could host. So that people signing up for a group could know ahead of time what to expect, I asked each facilitator to declare in advance whether the host home was fixed or would be rotated. (Geographic location and transportation were concerns for some participants.)

The period of a meeting
A two-hour timeframe has proven to be a viable period to meet in consideration of the purpose of the group and availability of participants, especially on a weeknight. Experience has shown that the Spiritual Life Dinner Group model presented here is a practicable way to achieve the sense of authentic community with weekly two-hour meetings over a period as short as five weeks.

How to provide for the meal
While it was left up to each group, it was suggested that each member bring something for the dinner and that a different person each week be responsible for the main dish, especially if all the meetings were to be in one host home. All the groups adopted this tactic. It worked well. Each week someone coordinated to ensure variety for the meal. Keep it simple; resist any temptation to make the group a gourmet dining club. Make it about creating authentic community. While dinner groups are popular, offering coffee, lunch, or dessert meetings may increase overall participation and provide the opportunity of authentic community and connection to more people.

What time to schedule the meeting

Rather than having a new group of eight people trying to agree on a time, I left it up to each group facilitator in collaboration with the host home to set the scheduled meeting time. The sign-up sheets then noted the day, time and location for each group. People looking for a group chose one based on their overall needs.

Wanting people to have spaciousness in their evening after the meeting, I set 6:00 p.m. as the start time of a Friday practice group. It simply didn't work because many in the group couldn't get there on time after their workday. We shifted the time to a half hour later. With the next week's meeting at an outlying location, we started at 7 p.m. to allow more time for people to travel the extra distance.

What to do if people are not there at the stated start time

Did I mention to begin on time? Starting and ending on time is important to the well-being of the group. Honoring the time commitment sets the tone and reinforces that *everyone matters*. (Remember how you felt when you went out of your way to arrive at a meeting on time only to wait fifteen minutes for latecomers to show up?) If the group does not adhere to beginning and ending times, then other parts of the structure will slip and the quality of the experience of participants will suffer. A lot needs to happen in two hours. *Start on time, end on time, have a meaningful time.*

Variety is the spice of life

Some creative people in our dinner groups have come up with ways to add variety to the basic meeting template. Here are a few ideas:

- Read a daily devotional aloud and invite a round of sharing about what that stirs in each person.

- Place a brief scripture passage beneath each placemat (or draw from a basket) and have each person read it aloud and share about how it relates to them.

- Ask participants to bring something meaningful to them and to share about it. It could be a photograph, memento, or something they have created or crafted, etc.

Delegating responsibility for portions of the meeting

The opening prayer, closing prayer and the coordination of logistics for the next meeting can be delegated early on. Facilitation of the table topics, the salon, and prayer support, however, require a little more skill and finesse. It is recommended that these roles be delegated only after a few meetings and only after appropriate discernment. If you do delegate, support each person with coaching before the meeting and by tracking time at the meeting.

Table topics and salon topics

With multiple rounds of groups over time, the same topics repeated may naturally lose their appeal.

Additional topics may be desired. Don't pick just any topic from a list of icebreakers in a book or from the internet. Make sure the topic is one that will likely stimulate responses that are personally relevant. Crafting new topics can be creative and fun. At the same time, this calls for discernment. Avoid narrow topics, complex topics and potentially controversial topics as these do not align with the purpose of inspiring connection. Do not use topics associated with church issues or concerns. If in doubt, have several people review the proposed topic to see whether it feels connecting, neutral, or polarizing.

After the scheduled meetings, then what?

After the designated number of meetings, a group may elect to meet once or twice more, perhaps after a short break.

Forming New Groups

In the spirit of open and accessible groups, existing groups are encouraged to celebrate their final meeting with group members encouraged to be catalysts for new groups or perhaps to train to be group facilitators. One way to provide some variety around the short term groups covered in this book is to launch them at least several times a year. Previous participants are encouraged to sign up for a new group rather than resuming an earlier group. Forming the groups anew each time they are offered makes for an open process, provides the opportunity for different people to connect with one another, and keeps groups from becoming stagnant or cliquish.

Affinity Groups

The reproducible framework of the dinner group model can be utilized in any affinity group (singles, couples, young adults, seniors, etc.) to create authentic community among its members.

Application to Other Groups

The organizing principle *everyone belongs, everyone matters, everyone is a contribution* and elements of the dinner group model can be used to promote authentic relationships in virtually any small group from bible study groups to the search committee, from the capital campaign team to the elders or church board. (See Part Two for how this has been applied to the book discussion group. See Part Three for how this has been used in onboarding a new minister.)

CHAPTER 11

WHY PARTICIPANTS LOVE THESE GROUPS

Here is what some participants in the initial round of Spiritual Life Dinner Groups at Unity Renaissance Chesapeake (Virginia), had to say:

"This was a great opportunity to know others more deeply—to learn and practice prayer in a safe, encouraging atmosphere. Non-judgmental give and take. Organized, easy to fit into program. Hosts kept to planned program, everyone could participate as they wanted or not."

"I am so glad that I participated in the Spiritual Life Dinner Group. Getting to know people more intimately and socially has enhanced my Sunday morning church experience. I look forward to meeting more people in future groups."

"I appreciate the community and buddy relationships. Some I will have for a lifetime."

"My group was a wonderful opportunity to get to know members of my church family on a more personal level. It was a great experience to pray for each other and bless each other prior to parting. It was just terrific."

"I found I really bonded with the people in my group and reached a level of intimacy or comfortability [sic] that I don't think I could have or would have achieved in another way - even knowing everyone in the group [before we started meeting]."

"It's like a spiritual gourmet club full of wonderful support. It was intimate. I really got to know people."

"I brought the energy of the group meeting home and it would stay with me for days."

"Groups and classes anchor people together in a special way. [This] potluck, sharing and praying together is the best."

"I enjoyed a feeling of peace and knowing that I was lifted in prayer constantly."

"I really liked the structure, arriving and leaving on time, prayer at the end. I liked having a meal, and having all share in the various parts of the meeting."

CHAPTER 12

FIVE KEYS TO SUCCESS

This Spiritual Life Dinner Group model, like all models, is imperfect. Nonetheless, it has proven effective in providing a venue for people to interact and co-create an experience of genuine community. How can this happen in new, short-term groups meeting weekly for two hours? There are five keys to success:

Intention There is a clear intention for the groups to foster authenticity and connection—publicized up-front so that everyone will know what to expect.

Training Facilitators are trained hands-on rather than in a class. They experience the process by participating in a group that cultivates its own authentic community by practicing and living the process.

Structure Written materials are provided to support hosts, facilitators, and group members. Facilitators know their structure and implement it in a way that is not distracting to group members.

Modeling Facilitators model the authenticity and relational presence they desire in their groups.

Shared Understanding Facilitators review the Group Agreement with each registrant ahead of time and with the group at the first meeting, gaining a shared understanding of how group members want to be together.

Not long after our first round of groups finished, I met a couple who was coordinating a small group ministry for another church. When I saw them again a month or so later, I inquired about their own group. They were at their wits' end. They were disheartened that one person was trying to use the group for therapy. Being off-purpose and lacking mutuality, the small group experience was tarnished for everyone else. That doesn't have to happen.

PART TWO

The Spiritual Discovery Book Group: Beyond Opinions

CHAPTER 13

INSPIRING CONNECTION IN A BOOK DISCUSSION GROUP

What did I get when the success of Spiritual Life Dinner Groups spilled over into a new minister's love of both books and small groups? An opportunity to revisit how to shape and manage a small group book discussion so that it inspires connection—to self, to others, to one's spiritual life.

Recently I had a call from a friend who was excited about a book discussion group in her church. Her voice quavered as she revealed that she had never felt so close to God. I was touched. After learning about the overall program, I inquired about the makeup of the group and engagement of participants. On average there were just over a dozen group members. She characterized five or six as talkers and the rest as observers. Other than introducing themselves on the first night, three people hadn't said anything even though they were midway through the program. That doesn't have to happen.

In some groups the discussion of material in the book can sometimes feel like debate, perhaps with a few "experts" holding forth with great passion while others mostly observe. Even with more balanced participation, the topic can often dominate, offering people little opportunity to contribute beyond their opinions about the subject and whether they agree or disagree with the author—or with one another. I recall what I learned in homiletics class: Until we talk about our spiritual journey, our understanding of it is incomplete. What is needed is a small group book discussion model that makes it easy for everyone to contribute—to talk their own spiritual lives.

We developed such a model by starting with the organizing principle: *Everyone belongs, everyone matters, everyone is a contribution.* Then we adapted some of the methodology of the dinner group model. In order to invite more attention on the personal spiritual journey of the group members—as opposed to analyzing or drilling down through the material in a book—we named our groups "Spiritual Discovery Book Groups" rather than the more common "Book Study Groups" or "Book Discussion Groups." Likewise, the publicity about the groups included that the purpose was not so much increased understanding of material in a book, but rather increased understanding of one's spiritual life.

The organization, launch and operation of these groups parallel those of the Spiritual Life Dinner Groups discussed in Part One of this book. The following chapter explains how to conduct a Spiritual Discovery Book Group meeting.

CHAPTER 14

FACILITATOR'S GUIDE: SPIRITUAL DISCOVERY BOOK GROUP

The meeting guide (Exhibit N: "Facilitator's Guide: Spiritual Discovery Book Group") is a one-page template listing a schedule of the elements of the basic two-hour meeting. The following description of the guide assumes that you know the rationale and process for the dinner groups as detailed in the Part One.

This template is primarily a tool for your use in planning so that the meeting flows seamlessly. During the meeting, it is a quick reference for you or an assistant to use in keeping on track. The guide is not intended for participants lest they become more present to it than to one another and to their experience. They will know what to expect in the meeting from your phone call after they signed up and from your written welcome message.

Keep in mind that in order to prioritize connection in the group, you yourself must prioritize relational presence rather than a task orientation. What this means in practice is recognizing that "structure" is something that you give yourself before the meeting, not something that you impose on the group. Giving yourself structure before the meeting results in more spaciousness during the meeting to be present to yourself and to others.

The following paragraphs describe each major element of a basic meeting.

Arrival
Arrive about fifteen minutes before the scheduled start time of the opening circle. Offer to help the host or hostess with any pre-meeting needs. Welcome arriving participants, and furnish them name tags.

Opening Prayer Circle
Consider asking a group member *well before the meeting* to come prepared to do opening prayer. Tasking someone else with this piece gets them active and contributing even before the book discussion starts. Don't hesitate to ask the new person or someone who is typically slow to speak up in a group. If they don't want to accept, they will decline. And they may appreciate the opportunity to break the speaking ice without the pressure of having to be spontaneous. Convene the circle on time.

Overview of the Meeting
Although participants will have registered and received information describing the group, take time to give a short overview of the meeting in order to put people at ease. Revisit the expectation that the book be a vehicle to encourage individual reflection and sharing of one's own experience on the spiritual quest. The more you disclose your own hopes, desires, and concerns about

facilitating the group, the more likely others will be willing to share genuinely. Let them know that as facilitator you will be sharing in the group like everyone else and that your role is to guide the process of being together. This is a segue to the group agreement.

Group Agreement
Facilitate a shared understanding of "how we want to be with one another." Be sure that it is understood that should things get off track, you are the one to call for realigning with the Group Agreement (Handout #1).

Reading
Use a reading or poem of no more than 150 words to ground the gathering. Inviting a group member in advance to contribute this gets them engaged. A recorded song or other short piece of music could be used as well.

Moment of Self-Awareness
Immediately follow the reading with a moment of silence for self-connection. (Some groups may invite brief reflections spawned by the reading).

One-Minute Check-in
In the Spiritual Discovery Book Group, check-in is important because of its role in getting group members talking about themselves, rather than just giving their opinion about something. Because the momentum of check-in will carry over to the book discussion portion of the meeting, the questions or prompts for check-in are crucial in setting the tone for self-reflection followed by self-disclosure. A popular check-in prompt is "How was your week?" I've used it many times. While this is an easy prompt to respond to, group members sometimes learn more about one another's pets, children, neighbors, coworkers and bosses than about each other. Included in the facilitator's guide is a baker's dozen check-in prompts that have proven to be more evocative. If you are facilitating, remember to join in the check-in as a member of the group.

Be prepared to help group members unpack any short responses. For example, say the prompt is: *Something I'm looking forward to.* And their response is: "I'm looking forward to visiting my brother." Then they stop. Because some people may pause to think before continuing, wait. When it seems that they are not going to add anything, invite them to "say more about that." Or ask "What about that is important to you?" Do something to elicit a more meaningful response, particularly if the person is one of the first to speak. If you move on to the next person without making this effort, the impetus for depthless sharing may take hold.

At least for the first few meetings, have two rounds of check-in. This will support people in feeling known and accepted, a prerequisite for having a sense of belonging and mattering. The resulting sharing during the book discussion will be richer and more personal. The one-minute time frame encourages people to zero in on what is important. It also precludes the telling of long stories.

Almost all of us seem to lose track of "one minute" when it's our turn to speak. Support group members by having them experience how long one minute actually is. See "Table Topics" in Chapter 5 for more on how to track time graciously.

Book Discussion: The Process

The difficulty in setting up group discussion is how to hear something from everyone without overly constraining those who may have a lot to say. One way to address this issue is to have two modes of sharing on a given discussion question. Here's how it works, based on the popular format of posing questions to the group. Introduce the first question. A question could be offered by simply asking it or having someone read aloud the associated paragraph or section of text. After a brief pause, call for a round of uninterrupted sharing of individual responses to the question where each person has about the same amount of time to speak. After all responses (including the facilitator's) are on the table, have a period of group discussion where group members dialogue at will. Remind people to speak to the entire group, not just to the facilitator or to the person who previously spoke. The facilitator may defer to others before joining the discussion. Before closing the group discussion, nudge anyone who has not spoken by making eye contact or prompting with something like: *What else can you add?*

Allowing up to two minutes for each uninterrupted individual share seems to be sufficient for most people to get to the heart of what they want to say. Allowing ten minutes for open discussion provides the opportunity for deeper reflection and discussion around emerging themes, as well as for group interaction. Should the energy wane before the target time, move on to the next question in order to hopefully reengage everyone. For each meeting, have available at least one more question than you think you'll need. If most group members seem energized around a given question, stay with it longer than planned rather than having a rigid schedule. Go with the energy of the group.

Book Discussion: The Questions

Crafting the questions to be posed in the meeting is vital in transforming what may ordinarily be an academic discussion into an engagement that inspires introspection and sharing around personal experience. For example, suppose material from the book is about compassion. An academic question might be: *What is your take on the author's story about compassion?* A question that is more evocative relative to an individual's personal experience on the subject is: *Recall a time when someone was compassionate towards you—what happened, how did you feel, how did that impact you?*

Provide the questions in writing in advance of the meeting so that participants might ponder them as they are reading the associated chapter in the book. This will support them in being able to contribute with more clarity and depth about how the material relates to their lives or how their lives relate to the material.

Book Discussion: Open Topics

After the prewritten questions are discussed, allow about fifteen minutes for open discussion of topics and questions raised by anyone in the group. Depending on the material in the book and the makeup of the group, this can be the liveliest part of the meeting. Always include this open topics segment for group members to contribute questions or discussion topics even if it means cutting short the discussion of the prewritten questions. Defer to the other group members, but be prepared with a few ideas just in case.

Feedback

After open topics and before closing the meeting, initiate a round of feedback. Keep it simple, such as: *What worked well in this meeting? What would make it more fulfilling?* To invite concise comments and avoid protracted discussion, some facilitators ask for the feedback in two sentences. Whether you use the two-sentence form or a more open form, keep it brief—a half-minute for each share. Listen to the suggestions for any themes or unmet needs that can be addressed by making shifts in the format or group process. But be aware of potential unintended consequences.

Closing

Remind or recruit volunteers to provide the opening prayer, a reading, and snack for the next meeting. Call on someone to lead a final prayer. Leave the host home or meeting place as a group.

(Options)

The three-part affirmative group prayer as discussed in Part One can be incorporated into the meeting in lieu of the usual closing prayer by one individual. People enjoy giving and receiving this prayer support. See "Prayer Support" in Chapter 5 for details.

Some groups have found it beneficial to add ten minutes or so of social time before or after each meeting. Some groups have snacks set out at the beginning of the gathering, others have a snack in the middle of the meeting. Many of the groups will decide to celebrate and have closure by having a meal or something special at or after the last meeting.

Bible Study

This Part Two was written in the context of a general book discussion group. The principles and elements of the process described are easily transferable to the traditional bible study group. The first step is to take your current meeting template or agenda and revise it to include some of the meeting elements already detailed in this book. (Record the current agenda in the left column of Handout #8; the revised agenda in the right column.) The elements which tend to be most supportive of creating authentic community are: icebreakers that evoke meaningful personal sharing (referred to as "table topics" in this book), deep sharing topics ("salon topics"), group prayer support (not just corporate prayer) that continues individually between meetings, and end-of-meeting feedback from each person on what is working well and what could be better. Of course, to be effective in building authentic community, any of these elements must be facilitated in a way that honors our universal need to feel safe, to belong, to matter, and to make a difference.

CHAPTER 15

TRAINING FACILITATORS

The purpose of training is twofold. First, to provide candidate facilitators hands-on practice in the process itself. Second, to have them encounter being in a group where participants share from their own experience, cares, and concerns instead of only voicing their views about a topic or taking a stand on an issue. Consequently, the format of the training is a mock meeting followed by practice in conducting portions of the meeting. The ideal group size is six to eight, the same as for a real group.

Interview candidate facilitators (see Exhibit J) and let them know what to expect regarding the training (see Exhibit O: "Facilitator Training: What to Expect").

The pre-work for the trainees is reading Part One of this book (in order to begin developing an understanding of why each element of the process is like it is), studying Part Two, and reading a designated chapter in the book that will be discussed in their groups (so that they might respond to a preselected question on the chapter during the training). The following discussion assumes that there are co-leaders of the training and that they have facilitated a Spiritual Life Dinner Group according to the methodology given in Part One. (Without a trainer experienced in the Part One dinner group process, the training group will be a co-learning, practice group similar to that described in Chapter 8.)

Using Exhibit P: "Facilitator Training: Trainer's Guide," the co-leaders allocate between them the various sections to be facilitated during the training. Roughly, the mock meeting can be divided into sections as follows:

> (a) Opening (Prayer, Overview, Reading, Self-Awareness)
> (b) Group Agreement
> (c) Check-in
> (d) Book Discussion: Prewritten Questions (Uninterrupted sharing, Group discussion)
> (e) Book Discussion: Open Topics
> (f) Feedback
> (g) Closing

The co-leaders facilitate the mock meeting as if it were a real group, pausing momentarily after each element or section, however, to debrief. They ask questions of the trainees to bring out the purpose of each element and the subtleties of how that element is introduced and implemented. Where appropriate, they focus on what not to do.

The amount of time for certain elements of the mock meeting is less than that for a real meeting. For example, after the uninterrupted individual sharing round is completed, there is only a few minutes of group discussion of the question selected. It isn't necessary to have the normal full ten minutes of discussion for the trainees to get the feel of the experience. Likewise, after the introduction of open topics, only a few minutes of discussion is needed as the important aspect is the setup. What is important for trainees to learn and practice is how to smoothly set up the individual sharing and then the group discussion. Their directions to the group need to be rich in context so that people can easily understand that what is being done is an expression of shared values: *Everyone belongs, everyone matters, everyone is a contribution.*

At the conclusion of the mock meeting, there is an overall debriefing. For questions and answers on the template for their group meeting, the facilitators-in-training are referred to Exhibit N: "Facilitator's Guide: Spiritual Discovery Book Group." This guide is structure for the facilitator in planning the meeting, not a handout for the participants in the group meeting.

The individual practice portion of the training begins after the mock meeting and review of the meeting guide are concluded. The elements which most influence the quality of the meeting are the ones for trainees to practice:

- Overview
- Group Agreement
- Check-in
- Book Discussion Question

There are two basic ways to proceed. One is to assume that an effective way of setting up each element was demonstrated in the mock meeting and that the trainees understood it enough to emulate it. A first volunteer acts as the facilitator and introduces the element and facilitates it just as if it were a real meeting. Afterwards, he or she is asked what they think they did well; what they might do differently. Feedback from a few trainees, moderated by the leader, in response to the question *"What might make that go over better in a group?"* reinforces the learning. Then another person plays the role of facilitator, and so on. One element at a time is practiced.

Another way to proceed is for a trainer to first briefly demonstrate the element (i.e., "this is how it is done"), then have each trainee emulate it and receive feedback. Each person will have his or her own style of providing the needed context of the element being practiced. By conducting the key elements of the meeting, facilitators will be more confident and at ease in their own first group meeting.

While skill in seamlessly introducing the elements of the meeting is essential for good facilitation, what is paramount is the consciousness of the facilitator and his or her ability to maintain relational presence no matter what happens in the group. It's not about getting through an agenda or checking "to do" items off a list. Creating authentic community is about holding the space for people to talk honestly about their own spiritual lives.

CHAPTER 16

LAUNCHING THE GROUPS

The launch of the book groups is similar to that of the dinner groups in Part One. In the publicity about the groups include Handout #6: "Frequently Asked Questions: Spiritual Discovery Book Groups" and Handout #7: "What to Expect in Your Spiritual Discovery Book Group." During sign ups, provide this information to each person registering for a group. After a pre-meeting phone conversation, facilitators send a confirming welcome message to group members. See Exhibit Q: "Sample Welcome Email Message: Spiritual Discovery Book Group."

In preparation for their first group meeting, facilitators utilize Exhibit R: "Facilitator's Checklist: Spiritual Discovery Book Group."

PART THREE

Inspiring Connection in Any Group

CHAPTER 17

THE SMALL GROUP IN ONBOARDING A NEW MINISTER

With discernment around what is most relevant, parts of the dinner group process may also be used in crafting a template for a series of single dinner meetings serving to support onboarding a new pastor (or even to strengthen connection within incumbent clergy). For larger churches, meetings would be mainly with staff and leaders; for smaller churches, with congregants.

I recently had the opportunity to participate in designing a small group model to meet the needs of our new minister for both connection and information. The minister was very interested in hearing directly from members about what was working well and what they would like to see changed. There was no shortage of ideas for meetings. Suggestions ranged from having groups of twenty or so people meeting with the minister during lunch after Sunday services to smaller groups meeting at a local restaurant. Based on experience with our Spiritual Life Dinner Groups, we opted for dinner groups of about eight people, each meeting once in a hosting congregant's home.

Again I turned to the unbeatable strategy of establishing a practicum group to do a practice run of the process and capture the lessons learned. It paid off handsomely. People who had volunteered to host the first rounds of our upcoming Meet the Minister Dinner Groups were invited to participate in the practice group. From the start we decided to focus on connection during the meal and to focus on gathering information in a sharing circle afterwards. In between would be a short, informal break for dessert and socializing.

The template for our meetings is included as Exhibit S: "Facilitator's Guide: Meet the Minister Dinner." This is specific to the dual purpose of our dinners—facilitating connection and gathering information on two specific aspects of our community: what's working and what needs improvement. If gathering information on a different aspect of your community is of interest, choose questions for the sharing circle portion of your meeting accordingly. If the primary purpose of your meetings is for people to get to know one another beyond just saying "Hi" after church services, choose topics and questions that are personal and support people in being seen and known. Draw on the table topics and salon topics included in the Appendix. Successful meetings don't happen by accident; planning and execution are required.

The key to having this work well is to inform participants at the start of the meeting as to the context for each of the major meeting segments so they will know what to expect. Otherwise, you will likely be faced with misplaced input (problem fixing and the like) at the dinner table and the challenge of reorienting the group around the intention of connection.

Along with the facilitators guide, the tips in the remainder of this chapter should help bring about success.

Preparation

- Recruit host homes and select dates well in advance.
- Publicize the purpose and context of the meetings.
- Have open sign ups so everyone will have equal opportunity to take part.
- Rather than promoting sign ups by functional group (e.g., board, choir, teachers), allow the opportunity for mixing.
- Shortly after the groups are formed on paper, the program coordinator or dinner home host sends each participant in his or her group "What to Expect from Your Meet the Minister Dinner." (Email or hard copy—see example below.)
- Host follows up with email one week in advance confirming attendance and coordinating potluck food items. Email embeds "What to Expect from Your Meet the Minister Dinner" text.
- The host follows up with phone calls to participants about five days before the scheduled meeting. (While this may seem redundant, if you don't over-communicate you will have no-shows.)
- The minister sends a "touch" email 2-3 days in advance of the meeting.

Managing Expectations: Sample Pre-meeting Email to Participants

SUBJECT: What to Expect from Your "Meet the Minister Dinner Meeting"

The meeting will start on time at 6:30 p.m. so arrive 10 - 15 min. early with your potluck item. I will contact you regarding what to bring. Note that this meeting is alcohol-free. Should you arrive after 6:30, come on in and join us at the table.

During dinner, you'll be invited to ask the Rev._____questions that are on your mind or in your heart. Also, you will have the opportunity to share a bit about yourself by responding briefly to a few table topics or questions designed to support connection with one another.

After dinner you'll be part of a sharing circle where each person in turn will respond in a few rounds of topics or questions. These responses will help Rev._____identify what is working in our church community as well as what changes might be beneficial. The focus is on providing concise information. This is not a problem solving session.

With a closing circle at about 8:30, the fellowship concludes and participants will leave in a group.

DAY/DATE/TIME: _____
HOST: _____
ADDRESS: _____
NEIGHBORHOOD: _____
HOST HOME PHONE: _____

Opening Circle

- Start on time.
- Acknowledge and explain the three roles: host, process keeper, minister.

Host:	Takes care of food and household logistics.
Process Keeper:	Supports the minister and participants in staying on track regarding the purpose of the meeting. Usually serves as the timekeeper. (Should be experienced in the methodology detailed in Part One of this book.)
Minister:	Models connection by personal sharing and being open to questions. Facilitates the sharing circle by posing topics or asking questions for each participant to respond to. Offers prayer support for each person.

Table Topics

- Minister covers sharing guidelines up front: about a minute to share on each topic, give headlines vs. story, and everyone listen and hold the space for the person sharing.
- Minister relates that time guidelines are to support equal sharing, conciseness, and ending the meeting on time.
- Minister emphasizes that this is about listening to the speaker.
- Process Keeper sets timer for one minute (smart phone with gentle tone works well).
- Minister announces a topic, invites response from each person in turn.
- Participant starts to close their remarks when the tone sounds (this is an invitation to close, not a demand). The minister moderates the sharing time.
- Process Keeper stands ready to intervene if the speaker gets off topic.

Prayer Support

- If the table topics include speaking about a personal challenge, the minister offers a brief word of prayer for each person concerning his or her challenge. Most people find this individual support to be very fulfilling

Sharing Circle

- Minister covers guidelines again and gives an option for follow-up at a later time if speaker has more to say than this venue supports (for example, meeting with the participant at a later time).
- This is a time for listening, not a time for problem-solving.
- The audible timer supports equal sharing.
- Minister moderates the sharing time.
- Process Keeper stands ready to intervene if the speaker gets off topic.

Closing Circle

- Participants offer a word of blessing for the minster. Close the meeting on time.

Managing the Process: Role of the Process Keeper

Because we recognized that the what-would-you-like-to-see-changed-in-the-church question had the potential of triggering unbridled expression, we included use of a digital timer with soft tone during the sharing circle portion of the practice group. We were hesitant to use the timer to moderate the sharing around the table topics during the meal. After all, the use of a timer seemed incongruent with our theme of connection while breaking bread. Therefore, we did not use the timer for table topics portion of the group. Again we experienced that few people have the ability to self-regulate when asked to speak for one minute. Because of that, the role of the process keeper in the upcoming real meetings was expanded to include tracking time for table topics as well as during the sharing circle.

Be direct and matter-of-fact when talking about using a timer to provide everyone an equal chance to share. While some will have initial resistance to timed sharing, everyone will easily recall their experience of being in a group which was hijacked by someone who passionately talked on and on, to the exclusion of almost everyone else. Acknowledge their concerns up front. Yes, they are the same ones you have—around rules vs. autonomy. Tell them of your positive experience of everyone having an equal opportunity to share as supported by using the timer in your practice group. Ask people to be willing to give it a try. At the end of the meeting ask for feedback on whether people felt they had an equal chance to be heard and get their point across.

In addition to watching time, the process keeper, along with the minister, is responsible for providing quick redirection when needed. The unsuspecting new minister may not be aware of the sensitivities and pain points of congregants. What may start out as an innocent statement from someone in the meeting can trigger an adverse reaction from a person who is carrying the belief of a past injustice suffered in church life. Here is an example from one of our meetings. A long-time member mentioned her view on the transition from one minister to another some twenty years ago. Another person jumped in to declare "No, that's not the way it was!" and started to offer proof, quickly shifting the focus from connection to *who's right, who's wrong*. At best such excursions set a problematic tone for the rest of the meeting; at worst they can sabotage the objective of the meeting. Therefore, the process keeper is obliged to interrupt as quickly as possible with something such as "I want to pause now. Let's go back to having one person at a time speak while everyone else listens."

If you have been a leader in church life very long, you probably have your own anecdotes that point to a compelling reason for having a process keeper for an onboarding meeting. A pastor new to the congregation may err on the side of being a gracious listener rather than inviting people to stick to the process designed to achieve the desired outcome of the meeting within the two-hour time frame. Without another person responsible or co-responsible for managing the process, the new minister, by default, is the traffic cop. And being new to the scene, the new minister will not be aware of some major potential pitfalls. Make it easy for the minister to be fully present to the people by installing a process keeper. If you've never heard of a process keeper, don't worry—I made it up. But do have one by whatever name.

CHAPTER 18

INSPIRING CONNECTION IN TASK-ORIENTED GROUPS

Task-oriented groups naturally tend to focus on the task at hand, consequently neglecting the one thing that could make a huge difference in their overall performance in the long run—connection. Most groups do attempt to address this by self-introductions and an icebreaker at the first meeting. Typically, however, these are weak relationship builders. Also, the usual check-in at periodic meetings is not very potent in forging lasting connections. In fact, even setting aside a significant portion of the first meeting for team-building activities is problematic because the task-driven people attracted to these groups are wanting to get to work. What is needed is the spaciousness to prioritize connection from the onset without the competing distraction of the awaiting task. The Spiritual Life Dinner Group fulfills this important need.

Build more enduring relationships by holding at least one such dinner meeting (or luncheon or dessert meeting) with committee or team members prior to starting the actual work of:

- building or expanding a facility
- drawing up a congregational covenant
- launching a capital campaign
- revising bylaws
- strategic planning, or conducting a minister search

The relatedness which is nurtured in the dinner meeting will serve to ground the group during times of challenge. It will anchor a sense of "we" in the face of strongly expressed opinions and preferences which tend to be divisive. In proposing one or more connection-focused meetings in advance of working meetings, be prepared for strong pushback from those who insist they need to get to work right away in order to get the job done. Stand firm—in the end they will thank you.

Use the basic template for the FIRST Spiritual Life Group Dinner meeting with some adjustments. Include a few more table topics and several more rounds of salon topics. This will extend the gathering by close to an hour.

Don't stop with a single dinner meeting. Once working sessions begin, allocate a portion at the start of each to give people the opportunity to be seen and heard beyond the task at hand. Use the table topics and salon topics as a resource from which to draw in order to move beyond a superficial check-in by inviting group members to share something personal and meaningful.

Table topics (evocative icebreakers), the salon (sharing circle), and affirmative prayer as taught in Part One can also be employed by boards, committees, or any group yearning to reap the benefits of a greater sense of connectedness as they prepare to undertake their work. By taking time to employ some of these methods in service of the universal need to belong and matter, the group will have the foundation to maintain cohesion even in times of great challenge. Use Handout #8 to revise any agenda to include elements designed to support authentic connection.

AFTERWORD

I hope this narrative of my stumbles and success in creating small groups where everyone matters has inspired you to a greater vision for your own groups. I would enjoy hearing about your experience as you initiate or refine your small group ministry, train group leaders, facilitate your own small group or apply the principles and practices of this work to conventional task-oriented groups and committees. You may reach me by email at eddieoliver@hotmail.com or through my website www.LifeGivingConversations.com. Meanwhile, so that other readers might better understand what this book is about, please post your review.

Eddie Oliver

Appendix

Exhibit A. Facilitator's Guide: FIRST Spiritual Life Dinner Group Meeting

hr:min	Meeting Element	Comments
	Arrive 30 min. before Opening Circle	Check with the hosts and offer support
	Welcome arriving members	Name tags
0:00	Opening Circle Check-in	*"How I am now (in this moment)?"* (1 or 2 sentences)
	Opening Prayer	Include those who have not yet arrived
0:05	Begin the Meal	
	Preview what the group will be doing during the meal; and your role	
	Table Topics—invite responses to the table topics. Each shares for about one minute on a topic; then move to the next round. Conversational.	*1. A brief introduction of me…* *2. What drew me to join this group* *3. Other than family, something that is currently bringing me joy*
0:40	Serve One Another (may be initiated before final table topic)	Have each person serve another person dessert
	Preview what the group will be doing after the 10 min. break	
0:50	Cleanup Break	Also allows time to socialize
1:00	Gather in the Sitting Area	Circular style seating so all can see, be seen
	How We Want to Be with One Another (Distribute copies of Handout #1: "Group Agreement")	Participants read sections in turn, with interactive discussion of what each item means, and what it would look like. Ask: *Are you willing to try this for our meetings?*
	The Salon	Explain how it works
	Reading for the Salon (Distribute copies of Exhibit B: "'On Listening' Article")	Review the article by having each participant read aloud a portion of "On Listening."
1:15	Salon Round 1 (2 min. each person)	Salon Topic: *A time I felt heard and understood*
1:35	Salon Round 2 (1 min. each person)	Salon Topic: *My experience of sharing with the group in the first round; of being the listener.*
1:45	Prayer Support (Distribute copies of Handout #2 "Affirmative Prayer Worksheet," 3x5 cards, pens)	Teach and participate in the three-column prayer. Each person takes away a card listing the prayer requests as a reminder of daily prayer for others in the group.
1:55	Arrangements for the Next Meeting	Date, time, place, provision for food
	Feedback Round on this Meeting	*What worked well?* *What would make our meeting more fulfilling?*
	Closing Circle	Brief prayer
2:00	Leave the host home as a group	
week	Daily prayer support—everyone	Use the 3x5 prayer request cards from this meeting

EXHIBIT B. "On Listening" Article

Spiritual Life Dinner Groups
Our Vision: Everyone is connected
OurMission: To enrich life, one small group at a time

They broke bread in their homes and ate together with glad and sincere hearts." Acts 2:46

On Listening by Ralph Roughton

When I ask you to listen to me and you start by giving advice, you have not done what I have asked.

When I ask you to listen to me and you begin to tell me why I shouldn't feel that way, you are trampling on my feelings.

When I ask you to listen to me and you feel you have to do something to solve my problem, you have failed me, strange as it may seem.

Listen! All I ask is that you listen, not talk or do - just hear me... I can do for myself. I'm not helpless. Maybe discouraged and faltering, but not helpless.

When you do something for me that I can and need to do for myself, you contribute to my fear and inadequacy.

But when you accept as simple fact that I do feel what I feel, no matter how irrational, then I can quit trying to convince you and get about the business of understanding what's behind this irrational feeling. And when that's clear, the answers are obvious and I don't need advice.

Irrational feelings make sense when we understand what's behind them.

Perhaps that's why prayer works, sometimes, for some people...because God is mute, and He doesn't give advice or try to fix things. God just listens and lets you work it out yourself.

So, please listen and just hear me. And if you want to talk, wait a minute for your turn, and I'll listen to you.

EXHIBIT C. Facilitator's Guide: SECOND Spiritual Life Dinner Group Meeting

hr:min	Meeting Element	Comments
	Arrive 30 min. before Opening Circle	Check in with the hosts and offer support
	Welcome arriving members	Name tags if needed
	Opening Circle Check-in	*"How I am now (in this moment)?"* (1 or 2 sentences)
0:00	Opening Prayer	Include those who have not yet arrived
0:05	Begin the Meal	
	Preview what the group will be doing during the meal; and your role	
	Table Topics. Invite responses to the table topics. Each shares for about one minute on a topic; then move to the next topic. Conversational.	*1. Where I grew up and a fond memory* *2. Something you may be surprised to know about me* *3. Something that is easy for me but may be a struggle for others and how that has shown up in my life*
0:40	Serve One Another (may be initiated before final table topic)	Have each person serve another person dessert
	Preview what the group will be doing after the 10 min. break	
0:50	Cleanup Break	Also allows time to informally socialize
1:00	Gather in the Sitting Area	Circular style seating so all can see, be seen
1:00	Prepare for the Salon	Reaffirm the intention of the salon: a time of genuine sharing and deep listening
1:05	Salon Round 1 (1 min. each person)	Salon Topic: *Praying daily for those in this group (or share about your prayer life)*
	Salon Round 2 (3 min. each person)	Salon Topic: *Something that is going well in my life; something that is a challenge.*
1:40	Prayer Support (Distribute copies of Handout #2: "Affirmative Prayer Worksheet," 3x5 cards, pens)	Review the process. Use worksheet if needed. **Invite consideration of requests around the challenges that were just shared in the Salon Round 2.** All take away a card listing the prayer requests as a reminder of daily prayer for others in the group.
1:55	Arrangements for the Next Meeting	Date, time, place, provision for food
	Feedback Round on this Meeting	*What worked well?* *What would make our meeting more fulfilling?*
	Closing Circle	Brief prayer
2:00	Leave the host home as a group	
week	Daily prayer support—everyone	Use the 3x5 prayer request cards from this meeting

EXHIBIT D. Facilitator's Guide: THIRD Spiritual Life Dinner Group Meeting

hr:min	Meeting Element	Comments
	Arrive 30 min. before the Opening Circle	Check with the hosts and offer support
	Welcome arriving members	
0:00	Opening Circle Check-in	*"How I am now (in this moment)?"* (1 or 2 sentences)
	Opening Prayer	Include those who have not yet arrived.
0:05	Begin the Meal	
	Table Topics—invite responses to three table topics. Each shares for about one minute on a topic; then move to the next topic. Conversational.	Choose three table topics from the list included in Exhibit E: "Table Topics (Evocative Icebreakers)"
0:40	Serve One Another (may be initiated before final table topic)	Have each person serve another person dessert
	Preview what the group will be doing after the 10 min. break	
0:50	Cleanup Break	Also allows time to informally socialize
1:00	Gather in the Sitting Area	Circular style seating so all can see, be seen
	Prepare for the Salon	Reaffirm the intention of the salon: a time for uninterrupted sharing and deep listening.
1:05	Salon Round 1 (1 min. each person)	Salon Topic: *What I am noticing about myself lately*
1:15	Salon Round 2 (3 min. each person)	Salon Topic: Choose a new salon topic from the list in Exhibit F: "Salon Topics (Deep Sharing)."
1:45	Prayer Support (Distribute 3x5 cards, pens)	All take away a card listing the prayer requests as a reminder of daily prayer for others in the group.
1:55	Arrangements for the Next Meeting	Date, time, place, provision for food
	Feedback Round on this Meeting	*What worked well?* *What would make our meeting more fulfilling?*
	Closing Circle	Brief prayer
2:00	Leave the host home as a group	
week	Daily prayer support—everyone	Use the 3x5 prayer request cards from this meeting

Exhibit E. <u>Table Topics (Evocative Icebreakers)</u>

A personal accomplishment that I'm proud of (other than family)

Answered prayer

How I have made a difference for someone

How I wound up at this church

How I wound up in this area, city or town

How it has been for me to pray daily for those in this group

How someone has recently contributed to my well-being

I admire people who

I have a tender spot for

If there were an extra week this year and money was of no
  concern, I would

My guilty pleasure is

My favorite hobbies

My biggest pet peeve

Something that is currently bringing me joy (other than family)

Something I'm looking forward to

Something that is easy for me but may be a struggle for others,
  and how that has shown up in my life

Something that is going well for me

Something that is a challenge for me

Something that is on my bucket list

Someone who inspires me

Something you may be surprised to know about me

The best thing that has happened to me lately

The one characteristic that unfailingly describes me

What drew me to join this group

What I do (or did) as a career or homemaker

What I do to relax

What others can count on me for

Where I grew up—and a fond memory

Exhibit F. <u>Salon Topics (Deep Sharing)</u>

A difficult decision

An early experience that shaped who I am

Connecting with others

If I had it to do over

My life purpose

My spiritual journey

Something I yearn for

Something that is stirring in me

Someone who shaped my life

The best advice I ever got

The spiritual principle that is calling for my awareness now

What success is for me

Who I came here to be

What being in this group has meant to me (option for last meeting)

EXHIBIT G. Steps to Self-Sustaining Groups

Step	Lead Time to Initiate the Task in Advance of the Starting Week of the Group Meetings	Task or Activity
1	12 weeks	Form a coordinating team
		Cast an inspiring vision and compelling mission for these in-home dinner, lunch or coffee groups
		Create or adopt a logo that reflects your theme
		Choose a name or theme
		Enroll stakeholders in the idea of starting Spiritual Life Dinner Group
2	11 weeks	Decide on a specific launch date for the groups and the number of weeks to meet
3	10 weeks	Release initial publicity (general information)
4	9 weeks	Call for group facilitators
5	8 weeks	Interview candidate facilitators
6	7 weeks	Conduct four-week facilitator training
7	5 weeks	Release details of meeting dates and times
8	4 weeks	Conduct Q&A sessions for people interested in a group
9	3 weeks	Conduct sign-up for participants
10	Week of 1st Mtg.	Speak with each facilitator to offer support
11	0	Start the group meetings
	Time after Groups Start Meeting	
12	1 week	Meet or teleconference with facilitators after the first week of meetings
13	At or after last meeting	Capture testimonials and feedback by internet or other survey
14	After last meeting	Obtain from current facilitators recommendations for facilitators for the next round
15	Ongoing	Integrate feedback and learning into plans for the next round

Spiritual Life Dinner Group

Our Vision: Everyone is connected
Our Mission: To enrich life, one small group at a time

"They broke bread in their homes and ate together with glad and sincere hearts."   Acts 2:46

Are you looking for meaningful connections on your spiritual path? A new small group ministry will soon be a reality in our church. Spiritual Life Dinner Groups of about eight people each will meet weekly for five weeks starting in October. At coffee, lunch, or dinner meetings in individual host homes, group members will gather to break bread and enjoy spiritual fellowship in a meeting environment designed to foster genuine community.

<u>Are you called to facilitate a Spiritual Life Dinner Group</u>?

Required training for this special lay ministry is a four-week practicum. Candidates will participate in a training group that will meet starting the week of August 15th. The training will be facilitated by Maria Garcia. See the display in the Narthex for details or contact John Smith at 555-555. Also there will be an open Question & Answer session the first Sunday in August at noon in classroom 4.

Exhibit I. Sample Facilitator Interview Sign-up Form

Spiritual Life Dinner Groups
Our Vision: Everyone is connected
Our Mission: To enrich life, one small group at a time

They broke bread in their homes and ate together with glad and sincere hearts." Acts 2:46

Are you called to facilitate a Spiritual Life Dinner Group? Required training for group facilitators is a four-week practicum. That is, candidates will participate in a Spiritual Life Dinner Group that will meet weekly starting August 15th. This practice group will be led by Maria Garcia. Questions & Answers meeting Sunday, August 1st at noon in the classroom 4.

Please contact me to schedule a group facilitator interview...

Name _____

Phone(s) _____

Best time to call _____

e-mail _____

Comments

_____

_____

_____

Place this completed form in the volunteer mailbox or turn it in at the office.

EXHIBIT J. Facilitator Interview Guide

What are you currently enjoying in your life?

What draws you to serve in small group ministry?

What small groups have you participated in? Your roles?

Tell me about a small group experience that has been the most fulfilling for you.
    (follow-up #1) What was it about the group that made your experience
         fulfilling?
    (follow-up #2) What was it <u>about you</u> that contributed to that experience?

Reflecting on our vision and mission statements, what comes up for you?

In your own words, what is the purpose of our Spiritual Life Dinner Groups?

Relative to Spiritual Life Dinner Groups, what is your greatest hope?

What is your greatest concern?

What are some ways to support balanced sharing in a group?

How do you see yourself handling conflict within a group?

Do you commit to having a personal conversation prior to the first meeting with those who sign up for your group so that they might better know what to expect and start connecting with you?

Is there any distraction in your personal life that might prevent you from being fully present for your group?

What else might be important for us to discuss?

Are you available for the days and times the practice group is scheduled?

Are you interested in being a host home for the practice group? _____
            Is there seating for 8 people for a meal? _____

Notes:

_____

_____

_____

EXHIBIT K. <u>Sample Meeting Venues Poster</u>

Spiritual Dinner Life Groups

Our Vision: Everyone is connected
Our Mission: To enrich life, one small group at a time

"They broke bread in their homes and ate together with glad and sincere hearts." Acts 2:46

Starting the week of October 6th, groups of eight people each will meet once a week for five weeks in this new small group ministry. The purpose of these in-home dinner, lunch, or coffee groups is to foster more meaningful connection among group members. The group process, guidelines, and facilitation style are designed to encourage equal, safe participation in each group. Everyone matters.

Participants will:

Break bread (serve one another) · Fellowship (enjoy one another)
Deeply Listen (hear one another) · Celebrate (affirm one another)
Pray (support one another)

See Program Flyers in the Narthex for Details. Sign-up period is from Sunday September, 14 through Sunday, September 28.   Contact the group facilitator or [insert program coordinator contact information here] for more information.

When	*Where Group will Meet*	*Facilitator*
Sunday Lunch	At the Church (Host Homes are Needed)	photo — *Facilitator's name*
Sunday Dinner	Virginia Beach Indian River Road	photo — *Facilitator's name*
Monday Morning Coffee	(Host Homes are Needed)	photo — *Facilitator's name*
Tuesday Dinner	Virginia Beach Larkspur	photo — *Facilitator's name*
Saturday Lunch	Chesapeake Great Bridge	photo — *Facilitator's name*

EXHIBIT L. <u>Checklist of Meeting Supplies</u>

____Roster for this Group (w/ phone numbers, e-mail addresses)

____Address and Directions to Host Home

____Phone Number for Host Home

____List of Food Assignments

____Name Tags, Marker

____"General Guidelines"

____"Facilitator's Guide" for Each Meeting

____Table Topics List

____Salon Topics List

____"Group Agreement" *

____"On Listening" Article *

____"Affirmative Prayer Worksheet" **

____3 x 5 Index Cards ***

____Pencils / Pens

____Timekeeping Device

_____

  * 8 copies, first meeting

 ** 8 copies, first two meetings

*** 8 for each meeting

EXHIBIT M. Participant Sign-up Sheet

Meet for Five Weeks	Meeting Time	Date of First Meeting	Host Home for First Meeting	Location of First Meeting	Notes
Saturday Lunch Group	noon – 2:00 p.m.	Oct. 12	Mary and John Smith (pet-free)	Chesapeake-Great Bridge *Facilitator will provide details*	Participants will share the provision of food and beverages

Facilitators: Mary and John Smith are excited to be involved in facilitating the Spiritual Life Dinner Groups because they love to develop connections with people that are based in real intimacy. "When we are open and pray with and for each other needs and desires the connections become deep and lasting. In this way we empower the faith of each group member as we get to share and experience the results of our prayers."

Name	Phone	E-mail Address	
1. John Smith	555-5555	jsmith@email.com	*Co-facilitators Host Home (Pet-Free)*
2. Jane Smith	555-5555	msmith@email.com	
3.			
4.			
5.			
6.			
7.			
8.			

EXHIBIT N. Facilitator's Guide: Spiritual Discovery Book Group

Book:_____Author:_____Chapter:_____Date:_____

hr:min	Meeting Element		Comments
	Welcome / Introductions		As members arrive - Nametags
Opening			
0:00	Opening Prayer		Include those who have not yet arrived
	Overview of Meeting		What we'll be doing in this meeting
	Reading		Brief reading (150 words or less) to ground the gathering
	Self-Awareness		Moment of silence
	Group Agreement		Invite reading in parts. *What would each look like?* Check on willingness to try this way of being together.
0:15	One-minute Check-in	Suggested prompts: *What drew me to join this group* *Something I'm looking forward to* *A brief introduction of me...* *Something I am are enjoying and why*	*What's going well in my life; what's challenging* *The best thing that has happened to me lately* *Where I grew up and a fond memory* *Someone who helped shape my life*
0:25	One-minute Check-in	*Something you may be surprised to know about me* *How someone has recently contributed to my well-being* *What is easy for me that may be a challenge for others & how that has shown up in my life*	*What others can count on me for* *I have a tender spot for*
Book Discussion – Individual Sharing & Group Discussion			
0:35	Question 1 (25 min.)		a. Uninterrupted sharing round (1-2 min. each person)
			b. 10 min. group discussion
1:00	Question 2 (25 min.)		a. Uninterrupted sharing round (1-2 min. each person)
			b. 10 min. group discussion
1:25	Snack & Stretch Break		
1:30	Open Topics (20 min.)		Group discussion of topics inspired by group members
Closing			
1:50	Feedback (½ min. each person)		*What worked well in this meeting?* *What might make our time together more fulfilling?*
	Closing Circle		Reminders: who is doing snack, reading and prayer for next meeting
	Closing Prayer		
2:00	Leave the host home as a group		

EXHIBIT O. Facilitator Training: What to Expect

Deliverables

Participants will gain skill and confidence in addressing typical concerns in having fulfilling groups: Starting and ending on time; all group members engaged and sharing; no one dominating the group; fostering authenticity; staying on topic.

Pre-work

Study Part One and Part Two of the reference text [this book]. In the book selected for the Spiritual Discovery Book Groups, read chapter _____ ahead of time in order to engage the training, part of which includes a mock Spiritual Discovery Book Group meeting where everyone responds to a question from the chapter. (We will not be reading the chapter at our training). One of the following questions will be asked:

1. _____
2. _____
3. _____

Mock Meeting

Conducted by the trainers, the mock meeting simulates the methodology of the Spiritual Discovery Book Group. Trainees experience the benefits of structure implemented in such a way that it is not distracting.

First Meetings: Why do some feel "stiff"?

Brainstorming and dialogue to address a common complaint.

Practice

Based on the required reading and experience of the mock meeting, each facilitator-in-training will practice "live" the parts of the Spiritual Discovery Book Group meeting which most contribute to the core needs of group members to belong, to matter, to contribute: Overview; Group Agreement, Check-in, and Book Discussion (Individual Sharing and Group Discussion). Included will be practice in tracking the time that individuals share during check-in and the uninterrupted sharing portion of book discussion.

Review of the Facilitator's Guide

Congregant Sign-Ups

Support for Facilitators

Concise and Meaningful Feedback

Exhibit P. Facilitator Training: Trainer's Guide

Mock Meeting

hr:min	Meeting Element		Comments
0:00	Opening Prayer		Include those who have not yet arrived
	Overview of Meeting		What we'll be doing in this meeting
	Reading		Brief reading (150 words or less) to ground the meeting
	Self-Awareness		Moment of Silence
0:25	Group Agreement		Invite reading in parts. *What would each look like?* Check on willingness to try this way of being together.
0:45	One-minute Check-in		*What's going well in my life; what's challenging*
1:05	Question from Selected Book	a. Uninterrupted sharing round (1 min. each person)	
		b. Group discussion (3 min.)	
1:25	Open Topics		Group discussion on topics inspired by group members (3 min.)
1:30	Feedback (½ min. each person)		*What worked well in this mock meeting (training)? What might make our time together more fulfilling?*
	Closing Circle		[in a real group meeting, logistics for the next meeting are covered]
1:35	Closing Prayer		

1:40	15 min. BREAK

Debrief and Review Supporting Materials

1:55	Debrief the Mock Meeting
2:05	Review the Facilitator's Meeting Guide, What to Expect from Your Spiritual Discovery Group, and the FAQs

Practice

2:25	Practice the Overview
2:40	Practice setting up the Group Agreement
3:10	Practice the Check-in
3:30	Practice the Book Discussion Question

3:45 -4:00	Debrief the Practice; Q&A

EXHIBIT Q. Sample Welcome Email Message: Spiritual Discovery Book Group

First Meeting: [time, day of week, date, place]

Dear [group member]

I am delighted that you have signed up for our Spiritual Discovery Book Group. I know we are going to have a rich and meaningful time together and I look forward to learning, growing and sharing with you. Until we talk about our spiritual journey, our real world understanding of it is incomplete. My role is not to teach or provide information but rather to facilitate—to make it easy for you to share your experience of your spiritual journey.

Please obtain a copy of the book and read Chapters_____in advance of our first meeting. We will draw on the questions included in your Participant Packet * to prompt the sharing in our group. If you did not get a hardcopy of the packet at registration, print out the attachment. Bring a copy of the Participant Packet with you.

Meeting place_____[address]
Directions _____
Group begins at_____ [time]
Group concludes at_____[time]

I am so looking forward to our time together. What a great group we have!

Joe Doe [list group members]
Joe Doe
Joe Doe
Joe Doe
Joe Doe
Joe Doe
Joe Doe
[include your name somewhere in this group list]

Should you arrive after the starting time, just come on in—we'll be saving a place for you. And let me know if you have any other questions (phone 555-5555).

[sign as you wish]

---

* The Participant Packet includes three handouts: Frequently Asked Questions, What to Expect in Your Spiritual Discovery Book Group, and a Schedule of Chapters from the book with a List of Questions for Each Meeting.

EXHIBIT R. <u>Facilitator's Checklist: Spiritual Discovery Book Group</u>

Before Congregant Sign Ups

____Notify program coordinators if you are unable to be present

____Verify that your contact information and meeting venue information to be given registrants is correct

____Be prepared to say "NO" to people desiring to enroll when your total group size reaches eight

Congregant Sign Ups

____Greet each one and ask what you can let them know about the groups

____Be clear that these are not drop-in groups; need their commitment to prioritize attendance

____Provide the sign-up sheet

____Verify legibility of their contact information

____Give them a Participant Packet; include your contact information and meeting venue details

____Express your desire to have a conversation with them with them about the group at a time when there is more spaciousness

____Schedule a phone call or ask best times to call (write it down/update your digital calendar)

____Ask them to review the Participant Packet before the phone call

____Stop registering people when your group size reaches eight total

Within a Few Days of Sign Ups

____Connect by phone with each person on your group list according to their preference

____Discuss their expectations, hopes and desires for the group; yours

____Confirm their commitment

____(Ask three people to provide the opening prayer, a reading or a closing prayer for the first meeting)

____Confirm day/time/location of the group meeting

____Offer to be contacted should any cares or concerns arise regarding the group

(continued next page...)

____Request to be immediately contacted should their situation change, making it impossible or a burden to be in the group

After Group Members Are Phoned (well before the first meeting)
____Email a welcome message which includes:
    ____your contact information
    ____meeting venue details/directions
    ____reference to the Participant Packet which has the Chapter schedule and Chapter Questions
    ____a list of people in the group

Before the First Meeting
____Become very familiar with the Meeting Template so that you can conduct the meeting in a way that the structure is almost invisible to group members; otherwise, it will feel regimented
____Know the key points you want to make in remarks about the Overview and Purpose of the group
____Know how you want to facilitate the review of the Group Agreement
____Know the key points you want to make in setting up the Individual Sharing and Group Discussion

At the First Meeting
____Provide name tags
____Begin on time
____At check-in support shared understanding of "one minute" by demonstrating with a soft-tone timer
____Invite everyone to speak to the group, not to one person in the group
____When you notice things getting off track, speak up and bring the process back into alignment with the Group Agreement
____Capture the feedback at the ending of the meeting–without evaluating or problem-solving. (Later, reflect on the feedback in considering how to make the next meeting more fulfilling for group members)
____End on time

EXHIBIT S. Facilitator's Guide: Meet the Minister Dinner

hr:min	Meeting Element	Comments
	Welcome arriving participants	Offer name tags
0:00	Opening Prayer Circle Minister: Speaks to the purpose of the meeting	Include those who have not yet arrived.
		Purpose is to get acquainted with one another over dinner; then meet in a circle to share what we envision for ourselves and our spiritual community.
0:05	Begin the meal	Minister's personal remarks
0:10	Minister responds to questions	
0:15	Table Topics	1st Round (1 minute): *How you found our church* 2nd Round (1 minute): *Something you may be surprised to know about me* 3rd Round (2 minute): *Something that is going well in my life right now; something that is a challenge.*
0:55	Prayer Support (Minister)	A word of prayer for each person around the challenge they mentioned
1:00	Dessert & Stretch Break	Clear the dinner plates. Dessert. Social conversation.
1:15	Sharing Circle Minister: Speaks to the purpose and scope of this segment. Offers context for sharing.	Gather in the sitting area Circular style seating so all can see, be seen (Comparable time for each person)
1:20	Question One (1-2 min. each)	*1. What gift or talent do you or would you most like to share with our church community?*
1:35	Question Two (1-2 min. each)	*2. What is the one thing about our church that you would never want to change? What is important to you about that?*
1:50	Question Three (Brief. Three or four sentences without problem-solving)	*3. What is the one thing about our church you wish you could change tomorrow?*
1:55	Minister's personal remarks	
1:58	Closing circle	Participants each offer a few words of blessing for the minister
2:00	Leave the host home as a group	

Handouts

Group Agreement

Living our core values: *Everyone belongs; everyone matters; everyone is a contribution.*

Shared Understanding of How We Want to Be with One Another

Support   I commit to faithful attendance and to arriving and departing the meetings at the scheduled times.

Respect   I contribute to connection by listening attentively to others while they are speaking and by getting to the heart of what matters when it's my turn.

Self-responsibility   I speak for myself only and only about my experience.

Acceptance   I accept each person in the group. I do not give them advice or try to "fix" them.

Trust   I hold in confidence what is said in the group.

Prayer Support   Between meetings, I pray daily on the prayer requests of others in the group.

Affirmative Prayer Worksheet*

My Name for God	Where God is	Affirmative Request, Desire, or Need for *Myself*
It is not I, but the Father	In heaven	that does the work (John 14:10)
God	in all things	prospers me
Holy Spirit	acting within me	illuminates my mind
Divine Love	expressing through me	fills me with joy
The prospering power of God	everywhere present	guides me to right employment
The Presence of Christ	in my life	Is the fulfillment of my every need

1. Using the examples, each one writes a 3-part prayer request **for himself or herself**.

2. One person speaks his or her affirmation out loud.

3. Everyone in the group visualizes it, holds it in prayer consciousness (allow some time for this, about fifteen seconds or so), and then in unison affirms the request when prompted by saying "Amen" or "And so it is" or similar close.

4. Continue one person at a time until each prayer is affirmed by the group.

* adapted from *Stretton Smith's 4T Prosperity Program, The 4T Publishing Company, Carmel, CA 1998*

General Guidelines for Spiritual Life Dinner Groups

Beginning and Ending

Opening and closing times are honored as scheduled. The duration of the gathering is two hours with all guests leaving the host home at the same time.

Schedule for a 6 p.m. Group	
5:45	Arrive at host home
6:00	Opening Circle, then Meal
6:50	Break
7:00	Salon
7:40	Prayer Support
7:55	Closing Circle
8:00	Guests depart host home

Breaking Bread

Participants provide food for the meal.

Fellowship

Participants arrive fifteen minutes before the opening circle to deliver food items and settle in. The meal follows brief check-in and prayer. A few light table topics prompt each person to share something about themselves in the spirit of getting to know one another. The facilitator ensures that all have an opportunity to contribute in a balanced way.

Salon

Intention and a short reading or meditation helps create sacred space for members to reflect and express from their heart around a topic or question provided by the facilitator. Each participant has the opportunity for uninterrupted sharing while others listen deeply. Listeners do not reassure or offer advice. Rather, the group facilitates each person's surrender to self-connection and honest expression. Any challenges or need for healing or positive desire will be addressed in prayer support which follows the salon. To ensure balance, respect, and trust, everyone supports the Group Agreement.

Prayer Support

At the first gathering, a simple yet powerful format to create a personal prayer statement will be taught. No one will be asked to pray out loud for another. Members will continue daily silent prayer for one another for the week.

Commitment

Participants commit to: following these guidelines, honoring the Group Agreement, maintaining confidentiality, praying daily in support of each member of the group, and being faithful in attendance by making the group a personal priority.

Frequently Asked Questions: Spiritual Life Dinner Groups

"I have not seen any reference to a book, video or study guide for the groups. Why not?" *The purpose of the groups is for members to develop more meaningful relationships with others on the spiritual path. Experience has shown that this happens when people co-create a safe environment and share about their lives and about what they value. Books and other media are often useful, but are not necessary.*

"I am new to the church. Will I fit in?"
Yes. Even people who have been around for years will find that in the group, they will, in many respects, be new to one another.

"I have tried groups before. Some people hogged the floor and others debated how to solve another participant's problems. These groups did not deliver on their promise to create genuine community and connection. How do I know that this will not happen with this group?"
The group process has been designed to support balanced participation. Group members respect one another by honoring the Group Agreement.

"Why so strict on starting/ending on time?"
The specific starting and ending times are publicized up front so that no one is surprised when the group begins and ends on time, i.e., when the Group Agreement is honored.

"What can I expect if I arrive after the starting time?"
First, know that you were included in the opening circle with prayer for your well-being and safety. Expect a place saved for you at the table where the meal is in progress. Expect to be warmly welcomed as everyone is grateful for your presence because it is difficult for them to connect with you if you are not there. (Don't expect the group to wait for you or to back up and start over.)

"I'd like to be in a group but I'm apprehensive about the prayer support part. I have never prayed out loud for a person in their presence. What should I do?"
Join a group and learn with others who share your concern. Your group facilitator will walk everyone through a simple three-step prayer, providing written examples to support each person in creating their own request which will be held in silence, then affirmed by the group. No one will be asked to pray out loud for another. Feedback from participants cites giving and receiving prayer support as the most fulfilling aspect of the groups.

Handout #4a. From *Inspiring Connection: Small Groups where Everyone Matters*
©2015 Eddie Oliver www.LifeGivingConversations.com

"What are the requirements for a host home?"
A candidate host home should be: conveniently located, free of distractions, quiet, odor-free, and able to seat eight people for a meal as well as to accommodate eight in a comfortable sitting space where all the participants can see one another. Transportation and parking options merit consideration. Handicapped accessibility is a plus.

"I'm allergic to cats/dogs. What should I do?"
Look for a group that meets in a cat-free, dog-free home.

"I'm on a special diet. What should I do?"
Inform the facilitator and the other participants. Bring a dish that you enjoy. Invite others to experiment. Look for a "vegan," "vegetarian" or similar special group.

"Is childcare provided?"
The groups meet in members' homes so the church does not provide childcare. However, members of your group may consider pooling resources to meet this need.

"A friend is going to be visiting me during the time of one of the meetings. May she attend?" Any request for guests should be put before the group.

"I want to be in a group but the only one offered at a time when I am available is already full. What can I do?"
Sign up on the wait list to let the program coordinator know of your interest. The number of groups offered is constrained by the availability of trained facilitators.

"How can I learn more about the groups before making the commitment to belong?"
Look for individuals wearing a Spiritual Life Dinner Group badge on Sunday mornings. Interview them. They have experienced being in a group. Many will be facilitating a new group.

"I heard that if you miss a meeting you are dropped from the group. Is that so?"
Participants commit to be faithful in attendance, i.e., to make the group a priority for the scheduled meetings. That said, life happens. Should you need to miss a meeting, please advise the facilitator or host so the group will not be anxious about you. The group will include you in prayer support until you return for the next meeting.

"I have concerns and questions not addressed here. Who can help me?"
Contact the facilitator of the group you are interested in or the program coordinator.

Participant Feedback Form

1. What were your expectations in joining a group?

    _____

    _____

    _____

2. In group meetings, what worked well for you?

    _____

    _____

    _____

3. What would have made group meetings better?

    _____

    _____

    _____

4. Please share anything else that might enhance the next round of groups:

    _____

    _____

    _____

5. If you would recommend being in a group to a friend, what one or two things would you like for them to know about these groups?

    _____

    _____

    _____

6. Who was your group facilitator?

    _____

    Today's Date _____

Handout #5. From *Inspiring Connection: Small Groups where Everyone Matters*
©2015 Eddie Oliver www.LifeGivingConversations.com

Frequently Asked Questions: Spiritual Discovery Book Groups

"What is the purpose of these groups?"
To help us discover spiritual truths, through personal reflection and group discussion, that guide and enrich our everyday experience of the sacred. Until we talk about our spiritual journey, our real world understanding of it is incomplete.

"How does it work?"
Groups of no more than eight meet weekly for two hours. Meetings include an opening prayer, a reading, and check-in. Having read the assigned chapters, participants take equal turns sharing their experience relative to a few questions designed to deepen their awareness of their own spiritual journey. Also after each question there is a time for open group discussion. There is also a time for participant-inspired topics.

"I have been disappointed with groups before. Some people hogged the floor and others debated how to solve another participant's problems. How do I know that this will not happen with this group?"
Facilitators have been trained in a group process designed to meet the needs of each person to belong and to matter. Each meeting has times for uninterrupted individual sharing as well as for group discussion. Participants uphold the Group Agreement in order to support respect and trust.

"What is the Group Agreement?"

Acceptance	I accept each person in the group. I do not give them advice or try to "fix" them.
Attendance	I commit to faithful attendance and to arriving and departing the meetings at the scheduled times.
Trust	I hold in confidence what is said in the group.
Respect	I contribute to connection by listening attentively to others while they are speaking and by getting to the heart of what matters when it's my turn.
Self-Responsibility	I speak for myself only and only about my experience.

"What can I expect if I arrive after the starting time?"
First, know that you were included in the opening circle with prayers for your well-being and safety. Expect to be welcomed as you join in. (Don't expect the group to wait for you or to start over).

"What about ending on time?"
Starting and ending times are publicized up front so that group members know what they are committing to and the host as well as host home is honored.

"I understand that these are not intended to be drop-in groups. How can I learn more before making the commitment to join?"
Contact the program coordinators [insert contact information].

What to Expect in Your Spiritual Discovery Book Group

The meeting will start on time so please arrive a few minutes early. Should you arrive after the starting time, go on in and join the group. If you cannot make the meeting, please phone your group facilitator ahead of time. Briefly, here's what to expect in your group experience:

Centering	Opening Prayer
Breaking Bread	Dessert or Snack
Grounding the Purpose of Our Group	Brief Reading or Poem
Self-Awareness	Check-in
Shared Understanding of How We Want to Be with One Another	Group Agreement
Spiritual Discovery	Individual Sharing & Group Discussion
Freedom	Open Topics Inspired by Group Members
Shared Leadership	Feedback—what worked well; what might be more fulfilling
Shared Responsibility	Sign-ups to provide snack, reading, opening/prayer for remaining meetings
Celebration	Closing Circle

After the 2-hour meeting, the group concludes and participants honor the host and each other by leaving as a group.

Please contact your facilitator with any cares or concerns.

Handout #7. From *Inspiring Connection: Small Groups where Everyone Matters*
©2015 Eddie Oliver www.LifeGivingConversations.com

Worksheet: Promote Connection in any Group
Meeting by Revising the Agenda

Current Meeting Agenda	Revised Meeting Agenda *Everyone belongs, everyone matters, everyone is a contribution*
• Start	• Start
•	•
•	•
•	•
•	•
•	•
•	•
•	•
•	•
•	•
•	•
• End	•
	•
	•
	• End

Handout #8. From *Inspiring Connection: Small Groups where Everyone Matters*
©2015 Eddie Oliver www.LifeGivingConversations.com

ENDNOTES

1. Rosenberg, Marshall. B., *Practical Spirituality: Reflections on the Spiritual Basis of Nonviolent Communication* (Encinitas, CA: PuddleDancer Press, 2005)

2. Rosenberg, Marshall. B., *Nonviolent Communication – A Language of Life* (Encinitas, CA: PuddleDancer Press, 2003)

3. Brown, Brené, *Daring Greatly: How the Courage to Be Vulnerable Transforms the Way We Live, Love, Parent, and Lead* (New York: Gotham Books, 2012)

4. Brown, Brené, *The Gifts of Imperfection: Let Go of Who You Think You're Supposed to Be and Embrace Who You Are* (Center City, MN: Hazelden, 2010)

5. Gordon, T., *Leader Effectiveness Training* (New York: Wyden Books, 1977)

6. Manning, W. and Suggs, B., "Empowering Life's Energies" Workshop (The Academy of Coaching Excellence, Sacramento, CA, April 2008)

7. *Stretton Smith's 4T Prosperity Program* (The 4T Publishing Company, Carmel, CA, 1998)

ACKNOWLEDGMENTS

I am grateful for the thoughtfulness of Pamela Denyes that led me to experience the Global Youth Village which in turn inspired my vision of small groups where everyone matters. Pamela and her husband Jim, a well-known leader and group facilitator, provided unconditional support in my quest for a self-sustaining group process. They were members of the practice groups from which the Spiritual Life Dinner Group framework evolved.

Also I want to acknowledge the support of Rev. Laura Barrett Bennett, former senior minister of Unity Renaissance Chesapeake, who encouraged me to initiate the experiment of enrolling fellow congregants in co-creating a new framework and practices for small groups. Ann DeMichael has been a steadfast friend and longtime collaborative partner in developing the practical group processes described in this book. She has a magical way of adding a compassionate touch to any activity, meeting or task.

Rev. Diane Scribner Clevenger (www.prayattentionministries.org) provided insightful coaching during the challenging stage of reshaping the initial draft of the manuscript. My daughter, Katherine, reviewed the manuscript-in-process with fresh, thoughtful, discerning eyes. Finally, I appreciate the patient ongoing support of Starr Janicki who contributed not only editorial assistance but also occasional reminders of the distinction between success and perfection. As a participant in several newly formed groups, her candid feedback prompted refinements of the group process and training of facilitators.

Made in the USA
San Bernardino, CA
30 August 2016